INDEX to SURNAMES in 1851 CENSUS for BANFFSHIRE

Volume 1

Marnoch, Forglen, Inverkeithny, Rothiemay

Indexed by
Margaret Shand

∠929·4

36 95 28

ISBN 0-947659-23-4

First published September 1993
by
Aberdeen & N.E. Scotland
Family History Society

printed by:-
RAINBOW ENTERPRISES,
        Unit 2, Saxbone Development Centre, Dyce, ABERDEEN

BANFFSHIRE CENSUS 1851 - INDEX

Compiled by Margaret Shand in 1990

NOTES

NAME

MC has been changed to MAC. in surnames to make one sequence.

Christian names such as Helen, Janet and Elizabeth have been made uniform according to modern spelling.

N.B. The surnames of BURNET, BARNET and BENNET were often difficult to distinquish, especially in Keith(BAN) Parish, District 3.

PLACE NAMES

The abbreviations for Counties are in accordance with those used in the Geneological Research Directory. Where there is no County, the place is in Banffshire or its location was not known.

Counties have been designated according to the map in the Gaskin Report of 1967 e.g. Boharm is in Banffshire and not Moray. This should enable a family historian to locate the parish or place according to modern boundaries and then, if necessary, trace the history of any border changes.

N.B. Sometimes, there is a Parish called RAFFAN designated in Banffshire. It is presumed that this is the Parish of RATHVEN and the spelling is phonetic according to local usage. It is not to be confused with the Parish of RATHEN in Aberdeenshire.

ENUMERATION BOOK NUMBERS

The following points should be noted:-

The numbering of the books of BOTRIPHNIE parish in the census was 4, 5 and 6 as they were added on to the BANFF parish. I have numbered them 1, 2, and 3 with the enumerator's numbers in brackets.

In RATHVEN Parish, Portknockie District, the 16th, 17th and 18th books have been numbered in the census as 5, 6, and 7. I have changed them in the index to their correct numerical order.

BOHARM Parish is in two parts each with 3 districts - BOHARM(Moray) and BOHARM(Banffshire). CABRACH is similarly divided into Banffshire and Aberdeenshire sections.

KEITH Parish is in two parts - two small districts are described as being in the County of Moray and the rest is considered as in Banffshire. Consequently, there are two numbering sequences.

KIRKMICHAEL Parish is also in two parts with the quod sacra parish of TOMINTOUL being in a separate sequence.

CLARITY

Where a name, place or age was not clear, there is a ?. Marnoch District 8 was particularly faint and difficult to read

COUNTY of BANFF

North Sea

Elginshire

Aberdeenshire

COUNTY	BOUNDARY	pre 1891
"	"	post 1891
CIVIL	PARISH	BOUNDARY
SETTLEMENT		

Map labels: Portknockie, Findochty, Cullen, Sandend, Portsoy, Whitehills, Macduff, Gardenstow, Buckie, Portgordon, CULLEN, Banff, BOYNDIE, GAMRIE, RATHVEN, FORDYCE, BANFF, DESKFORD, Cornhill, ALVAH, KING EDWARD, BELLIE, ORDIQUHILL, MARNOCH, Keith, GRANGE, Aberchirder, FORGLEN, ROTHES, KEITH, ROTHIEMAY, TURRIFF, BOHARM, BOTRIPHNIE, INVERKEITHNY, Craigellachie, CAIRNIE, Aberlour, Dufftown, HUNTLY, FORGUE, KNOCKANDO, AUCHTERLESS, ABERLOUR, GLASS, MORTLACH, GARTLY, CROMDALE INVERALLAN AND ADVIE, RHYNIE, CABRACH, AUCHINDOIR AND KEARN, INVERAVON, Tomintoul, GLENBUCHAT, KILDRUMMY, KIRKMICHAEL, TOWIE, STRATHDON, CRATHIE AND BRAEMAR, NORTH

Many Boundary changes have taken place both before and after 1851 the main bulk of which is covered in the publication :-"Boundaries of Counties and Parishes in Scotland as settled by the Boundaries Commissioners under the Local Government (Scot.) Act 1889" by Hay Shennan, and the said Act came into effect on 15th May 1891

The following extract gives the information used to create this map and shows the boundaries as they existed before and after 1891.

Extract :- The County of Banff had four detached parts, (not shown on map) surrounded by the County of Aberdeen viz, the parish of St. Fergus, and parts of the parished of Gartly, New Macher and Old Deer. On the other hand, it contained a detached part of the County of Aberdeen, which was at the same time a detached part of the parish of King Edward. Four other parishes (Cabrach, Cairnie, Glass and Keith) were situated partly in the county of Aberdeen and partly in the county of Banff, and five parishes (Belie, Boharm, Inveravon, Keith and Rothes) partly in the county of Banff and partly in the county of Elgin. Further, the parishes of Gamrie and Inverkeithny and parts of the parishes of Alvah and Rothiemay (all Banffshire parishes) were for certain purposes of administration held to form part of the county of Aberdeen.

SURNAME	CHR. NAME	AGE	BIRTH PLACE	CENSUS PARISH	BOOK	PG
ADAM	Alexander	10	Boyndie	Marnoch	9	4
ADAM	Ann	4	Banff	Marnoch	7	1
ADAM	Barbara	28	Forgue ABD	Inverkeithny	2	3
ADAM	Barbara	1	Inverkeithny	Inverkeithny	2	3
ADAM	Charlotte	29	Woolwich KEN	Marnoch	6	26
ADAM	George	6	Marnoch	Marnoch	6	15
ADAM	Grace	66	Forglen	Forglen	4	7
ADAM	Helen	6	King Edward ABD	Marnoch	6	6
ADAM	Isabel	71	Marnoch	Marnoch	5	20
ADAM	James	24	Marnoch	Marnoch	8	5
ADAM	Jane	74	Marnoch	Marnoch	6	22
ADAM	Jean	44	Marnoch	Marnoch	5	8
ADAM	John	18	Aberdeen ABD	Forglen	4	7
ADAM	John	37	Huntly ABD	Marnoch	1	1
ADAM	John	48	Marnoch	Marnoch	3	3
ADAM	John B.	3	Huntly ABD	Inverkeithny	2	3
ADAM	Margaret	14	Forgue ABD	Marnoch	7	1
ADAM	Margaret	58	Marnoch	Marnoch	1	11
ADAM	Margaret	44	England	Marnoch	7	1
ADAM	Margaret	18	Marnoch	Marnoch	5	25
ADAM	Margaret	69	Marnoch	Inverkeithny	1	9
ADAM	Margaret	23	Marnoch	Inverkeithny	3	6
ADAM	Mary	9	Marnoch	Marnoch	5	25
ADAM	Mary	14	Forgue ABD	Inverkeithny	1	3
ADAM	William	8	Marnoch	Marnoch	6	15
ADAM	William	71	Marnoch	Marnoch	6	22
ADAM	William	5	Forgue ABD	Inverkeithny	2	3
ADAM	William	27	Huntly ABD	Inverkeithny	2	3
ADAMS	James	25	Edinkillie MOR	Forglen	1	5
ADAMSON	Jessie	16	Marnoch	Marnoch	4	11
ADAMSON	Margaret	27	Marnoch	Marnoch	4	11
ADAMSON	Mary	54	Jamaica-Brit.subject	Marnoch	4	11
ADAMSON	Mary	25	Marnoch	Marnoch	4	11
ADAMSON	William	55	New Deer ABD	Marnoch	4	11
AITKEN	James	13	Marnoch	Marnoch	8	8
AITKEN	Robert	15	Fordyce	Marnoch	1	1
ALDER	William	17	Olney CAI	Forglen	3	8
ALEXANDER	Garden	67	Auchterless ABD	Marnoch	6	28
ALEXANDER	James	50	Culsalmond ABD	Marnoch	6	15
ALEXANDER	James	10	Forgue ABD	Marnoch	5	14
ALEXANDER	James	2	Marnoch	Marnoch	6	1
ALEXANDER	James	26	Inverkeithny	Inverkeithny	3	8
ALEXANDER	Jane	55	Culsalmond ABD	Marnoch	6	16
ALEXANDER	Janet	78	Auchterless ABD	Marnoch	6	28
ALEXANDER	Jean	7	Marnoch	Marnoch	6	22
ALEXANDER	John	76	Auchterless ABD	Marnoch	6	19
ALEXANDER	John	41	Marnoch	Marnoch	6	12
ALEXANDER	Margaret	1	Marnoch	Marnoch	5	14
ALEXANDER	Margaret	29	Monquhitter ABD	Marnoch	6	12
ALEXANDER	Mary	35	Marnoch	Marnoch	5	14
ALEXANDER	Mary	65	Marnoch	Inverkeithny	2	9
ALEXANDER	Robert	5	Marnoch	Marnoch	5	14
ALEXANDER	William	1	Marnoch	Marnoch	5	20
ALEXANDER	William	14	Marnoch	Marnoch	9	9
ALEXANDER	William	68	Inverkeithny	Inverkeithny	2	9
ALEXANDER	William M.	1	Forglen	Marnoch	8	11
ALLAN	Alexander	4	Marnoch	Marnoch	3	1
ALLAN	Alexander	1	Marnoch	Marnoch	5	6
ALLAN	Alexander	1	Marnoch	Marnoch	5	7
ALLAN	Alexander	3	Marnoch	Marnoch	5	17
ALLAN	Alexander	32	Marnoch	Marnoch	6	18
ALLAN	Alexander	4	Marnoch	Marnoch	8	10
ALLAN	Alexander	43	Rothiemay	Marnoch	3	1
ALLAN	Alexander	36	Marnoch	Inverkeithny	3	15

SURNAME	CHR. NAME	AGE	BIRTH PLACE	CENSUS PARISH	BOOK	PG
ALLAN	Alexander	29	Inverkeithny	Inverkeithny	2	3
ALLAN	Ann	11	Marnoch	Marnoch	5	7
ALLAN	Ann	30	Marnoch	Marnoch	5	22
ALLAN	Ann	46	Oyne ABD	Marnoch	8	9
ALLAN	Ann	25	Rayne ABD	Marnoch	5	6
ALLAN	Ann	20	Forgue ABD	Marnoch	9	1
ALLAN	Ann	66	Fintray ABD	Marnoch	5	22
ALLAN	Ann	37	Marnoch	Marnoch	4	1
ALLAN	Ann	51	Aberdeen ABD	Inverkeithny	1	1
ALLAN	Ann	12	Fordyce	Inverkeithny	3	15
ALLAN	Barbara	1	Turriff ABD	Inverkeithny	3	15
ALLAN	Barbara G.	1	Inverkeithny	Inverkeithny	2	3
ALLAN	Catherine	82	Marnoch	Marnoch	6	18
ALLAN	Catherine	28	Drumblade ABD	Inverkeithny	2	3
ALLAN	Catherine G.	5	Banff	Inverkeithny	2	3
ALLAN	David	13	Marnoch	Marnoch	4	1
ALLAN	David	5	Marnoch	Marnoch	5	7
ALLAN	Elizabeth	55	Marnoch	Marnoch	6	20
ALLAN	Elspet	29	Forglen	Marnoch	5	17
ALLAN	Elspet S.	20	Marnoch	Marnoch	4	1
ALLAN	George	47	Rayne ABD	Marnoch	8	9
ALLAN	George	11	Auchterless ABD	Marnoch	8	9
ALLAN	George	11	Marnoch	Marnoch	4	16
ALLAN	George	81	Marnoch	Marnoch	6	2
ALLAN	George	41	Marnoch	Marnoch	6	2
ALLAN	Helen	35	Forgue ABD	Inverkeithny	3	15
ALLAN	Helen	5	King Edward ABD	Inverkeithny	3	8
ALLAN	Helen	3	Turriff ABD	Inverkeithny	3	15
ALLAN	Isabella	8	Huntly ABD	Marnoch	3	1
ALLAN	Isabella	72	Marnoch	Marnoch	5	6
ALLAN	Isobel	78	Marnoch	Marnoch	6	2
ALLAN	James	12	Alvah	Marnoch	7	12
ALLAN	James	81	Banff	Marnoch	6	18
ALLAN	James	14	Forgue ABD	Marnoch	4	11
ALLAN	James	50	Marnoch	Marnoch	3	1
ALLAN	James	3	Marnoch	Marnoch	3	1
ALLAN	James	43	Marnoch	Marnoch	4	16
ALLAN	James	13	Marnoch	Marnoch	4	16
ALLAN	James	18	Marnoch	Marnoch	5	7
ALLAN	James	7	Fordyce	Inverkeithny	3	15
ALLAN	Jane	5	Marnoch	Marnoch	3	10
ALLAN	Jane	16	Marnoch	Marnoch	5	7
ALLAN	Jane	21	Marnoch	Inverkeithny	1	1
ALLAN	Jane W.	6	Banff	Inverkeithny	2	3
ALLAN	Janet	85	Deskford	Marnoch	5	13
ALLAN	Janet	46	Marnoch	Marnoch	5	13
ALLAN	Jean	10	Huntly ABD	Marnoch	3	1
ALLAN	Jean	20	Forgue ABD	Inverkeithny	3	10
ALLAN	Jean	72	Marnoch	Inverkeithny	2	9
ALLAN	John	9	Auchterless ABD	Marnoch	8	9
ALLAN	John	5	Forglen	Inverkeithny	3	15
ALLAN	Joseph	35	Marnoch	Marnoch	5	22
ALLAN	Margaret	50	Aberlemny FORFAR	Marnoch	8	10
ALLAN	Margaret	56	Auchterless ABD	Forglen	2	4
ALLAN	Margaret	39	Marnoch	Marnoch	4	16
ALLAN	Margaret	2	Marnoch	Marnoch	4	16
ALLAN	Margaret	7	Marnoch	Marnoch	5	7
ALLAN	Mary	7	Marnoch	Marnoch	3	10
ALLAN	Mary	18	Marnoch	Marnoch	4	1
ALLAN	Mary	4	Marnoch	Marnoch	4	16
ALLAN	Mary	29	Turriff ABD	Marnoch	3	1
ALLAN	Mary	3	King Edward ABD	Inverkeithny	3	8
ALLAN	Peter	40	Ordiquhill	Marnoch	5	7
ALLAN	Peter	14	Marnoch	Marnoch	4	18

SURNAME	CHR. NAME	AGE	BIRTH PLACE	CENSUS PARISH	BOOK	PG
ALLAN	Robert	7mths	Marnoch	Marnoch	3	2
ALLAN	Sarah	34	Marnoch	Marnoch	6	2
ALLAN	Sarah Ann	3	Marnoch	Marnoch	5	6
ALLAN	William	7	Auchterless ABD	Marnoch	8	10
ALLAN	William	16	Forgue ABD	Marnoch	5	22
ALLAN	William	6	Huntly ABD	Marnoch	3	1
ALLAN	William	2	Marnoch	Marnoch	3	2
ALLAN	William	70	Marnoch	Marnoch	4	1
ALLAN	William	29	Marnoch	Marnoch	5	6
ALLAN	William	41	Marnoch	Marnoch	6	18
ALLAN	William	56	Rayne ABD	Forglen	2	4
ALLAN	William	40	Inverkeithny	Inverkeithny	2	9
ALLAN	William A.	3	Banff	Inverkeithny	2	3
ALLAN	female	1	King Edward ABD	Inverkeithny	3	8
ALLEN	Jean	40	Marnoch	Marnoch	5	25
ALVES	Janet	43	Bervie KCD	Forglen	2	10
ALVES	Jessie	11	Marnoch	Forglen	2	10
ALVES	William	44	Durris KCD	Forglen	2	10
ALVES	William	14	Logie Buchan ABD	Forglen	2	10
ANAND	John	21	Bellie ABD	Forglen	3	1
ANDERSON	Alexander	2	Marnoch	Marnoch	6	21
ANDERSON	Alexander	40	Aberdeen ABD	Marnoch	1	13
ANDERSON	Alexander	7	Marnoch	Marnoch	2	3
ANDERSON	Alexander	16	Marnoch	Marnoch	2	12
ANDERSON	Alexander	1	Marnoch	Marnoch	6	8
ANDERSON	Alexander	1	Forgue ABD	Inverkeithny	2	14
ANDERSON	Alexander T.	6	England	Marnoch	1	13
ANDERSON	Ann	30	England	Marnoch	1	13
ANDERSON	Anne	4	Marnoch	Marnoch	6	7
ANDERSON	Annie	39	Marnoch	Marnoch	6	7
ANDERSON	Bell	16	Marnoch	Marnoch	8	11
ANDERSON	Betty	14	Marnoch	Marnoch	6	4
ANDERSON	Betty	36	Marnoch	Marnoch	3	10
ANDERSON	Catherine	46	Marnoch	Marnoch	5	25
ANDERSON	Catherine	25	Marnoch	Marnoch	6	3
ANDERSON	Catherine	23	Monymusk ABD	Inverkeithny	2	14
ANDERSON	Charles	2	Fochabers MOR	Marnoch	1	13
ANDERSON	Charlotte	11	Marnoch	Marnoch	6	21
ANDERSON	Christian	3	Marnoch	Marnoch	3	11
ANDERSON	Christian	9mths	Inverkeithny	Inverkeithny	3	8
ANDERSON	Christian	34	Boyndie	Inverkeithny	3	8
ANDERSON	Elizabeth	8	Marnoch	Marnoch	6	5
ANDERSON	Elizabeth	37	Ordiquhill	Inverkeithny	2	15
ANDERSON	Elspet	63	Rayne ABD	Marnoch	1	9
ANDERSON	George	4	Aberdeen ABD	Marnoch	1	13
ANDERSON	George	13	Forgue ABD	Forglen	1	1
ANDERSON	George	5	Marnoch	Marnoch	3	10
ANDERSON	George	38	Marnoch	Marnoch	6	7
ANDERSON	George	10	Marnoch	Marnoch	6	7
ANDERSON	George	88	Inverkeithny	Inverkeithny	3	9
ANDERSON	George	55	Inverkeithny	Inverkeithny	3	9
ANDERSON	George	20	Inverkeithny	Inverkeithny	3	9
ANDERSON	Helen	14	Marnoch	Marnoch	2	8
ANDERSON	Helen	44	Marnoch	Marnoch	3	10
ANDERSON	Helen	67	Marnoch	Marnoch	3	10
ANDERSON	Helen	55	Fordyce	Marnoch	6	20
ANDERSON	Helen	43	Keith	Marnoch	2	3
ANDERSON	Isabel	27	Marnoch	Marnoch	5	4
ANDERSON	Isabella	45	Auchterless ABD	Forglen	2	6
ANDERSON	Isabella	15	Forgue ABD	Forglen	2	6
ANDERSON	Isobel	37	Botriphnie	Marnoch	2	5
ANDERSON	Isobel	35	Marnoch	Marnoch	4	13
ANDERSON	James	5	Marnoch	Marnoch	2	3
ANDERSON	James	8mths	Marnoch	Marnoch	6	8

SURNAME	CHR. NAME	AGE	BIRTH PLACE	CENSUS PARISH	BOOK	PG
ANDERSON	James	40	Inveravon	Marnoch	2	3
ANDERSON	James	31	Forgue ABD	Forglen	2	6
ANDERSON	James	18	Aberdeen ABD	Marnoch	9	9
ANDERSON	James	16	Marnoch	Marnoch	6	21
ANDERSON	James	3	Inverkeithny	Inverkeithny	3	9
ANDERSON	James	12	Forgue ABD	Inverkeithny	3	8
ANDERSON	James	15	Fyvie ABD	Inverkeithny	2	14
ANDERSON	James	35	Forgue ABD	Inverkeithny	2	14
ANDERSON	Jane	1	Marnoch	Marnoch	3	11
ANDERSON	Jane	11	Marnoch	Marnoch	3	17
ANDERSON	Janet	13	Marnoch	Marnoch	3	10
ANDERSON	Jean	24	Marnoch	Marnoch	5	8
ANDERSON	Jean	52	Marnoch	Marnoch	6	3
ANDERSON	Jean	?	Culsalmond ABD	Inverkeithny	2	17
ANDERSON	John	10	Cairnie ABD	Marnoch	3	12
ANDERSON	John	5	Forglen	Forglen	2	6
ANDERSON	John	48	Marnoch	Marnoch	6	4
ANDERSON	Margaret	12	Marnoch	Marnoch	6	5
ANDERSON	Margaret	8	Marnoch	Marnoch	6	21
ANDERSON	Margaret	61	Drumblade ABD	Marnoch	6	12
ANDERSON	Margaret	9	Marnoch	Marnoch	3	10
ANDERSON	Margaret	67	Forgue ABD	Inverkeithny	2	15
ANDERSON	Margaret	6	Inverkeithny	Inverkeithny	3	8
ANDERSON	Margaret	52	Auchterless ABD	Inverkeithny	3	1
ANDERSON	Mary	5	Marnoch	Marnoch	6	5
ANDERSON	Mary	8	Marnoch	Marnoch	6	7
ANDERSON	Mary	36	Marnoch	Marnoch	6	21
ANDERSON	Mary Muir	7mths	Inverkeithny	Inverkeithny	2	16
ANDERSON	Peter	18	Marnoch	Marnoch	1	13
ANDERSON	Peter	76	Marnoch	Marnoch	3	10
ANDERSON	Peter	52	Marnoch	Marnoch	3	10
ANDERSON	Peter	5	Marnoch	Marnoch	4	13
ANDERSON	Peter	5	Inverkeithny	Inverkeithny	3	8
ANDERSON	Peter	33	Inverkeithny	Inverkeithny	3	9
ANDERSON	Robert	66	Drumblade ABD	Marnoch	6	12
ANDERSON	Robert	10	Forgue ABD	Forglen	2	6
ANDERSON	Robert	3	Marnoch	Marnoch	2	3
ANDERSON	Robert	32	Urquhart MOR	Marnoch	2	5
ANDERSON	Sally	14	Inverkeithny	Inverkeithny	3	9
ANDERSON	William	42	Marnoch	Marnoch	4	13
ANDERSON	William	50	Marnoch	Marnoch	6	3
ANDERSON	William	40	Fordyce	Marnoch	6	21
ANDERSON	William	17	Marnoch	Marnoch	6	4
ANDERSON	William	8	Forgue ABD	Forglen	2	6
ANDERSON	William	31	Inverkeithny	Inverkeithny	3	8
ANDERSON	William	31	Rayne ABD	Inverkeithny	2	17
ANDERSON	William	4	Culsalmond ABD	Inverkeithny	2	17
ANDERSON	george	4	Marnoch	Marnoch	6	21
ANDREW	Agnes	29	Marnoch	Marnoch	6	20
ANDREW	Agnes	33	Alvah	Inverkeithny	1	9
ANDREW	Agnes	68	Marnoch	Inverkeithny	1	9
ANDREW	Alexander	17	Inverkeithny	Marnoch	4	7
ANDREW	Alexander	36	Fordyce	Inverkeithny	3	13
ANDREW	Alexander	77	Grange	Inverkeithny	3	13
ANDREW	Ann	6	Forglen	Forglen	4	8
ANDREW	David H.	1	Marnoch	Marnoch	4	7
ANDREW	George	5	Marnoch	Forglen	4	5
ANDREW	George	8	Marnoch	Marnoch	4	7
ANDREW	Helen	20	Culsalmond ABD	Marnoch	4	7
ANDREW	Isabel	15	Alvah	Forglen	4	5
ANDREW	Isabel	62	Fordyce	Inverkeithny	3	13
ANDREW	Isabella	19	Inverkeithny	Marnoch	4	7
ANDREW	James	30	Inverkeithny	Marnoch	4	14
ANDREW	James	13	Marnoch	Marnoch	4	7

SURNAME	CHR. NAME	AGE	BIRTH PLACE	CENSUS PARISH	BOOK	PG
ANDREW	James	52	Marnoch	Marnoch	4	7
ANDREW	James	58	Alvah	Forglen	4	5
ANDREW	James	33	Fordyce	Forglen	4	5
ANDREW	James	1	Gamrie	Marnoch	5	15
ANDREW	James	64	Inverkeithny	Marnoch	4	3
ANDREW	Jean	42	Cairnie BAN	Marnoch	4	7
ANDREW	Jean	15	Marnoch	Marnoch	4	7
ANDREW	John	22	Alvah	Forglen	4	7
ANDREW	Margaret	40	Forgue ABD	Inverkeithny	3	13
ANDREW	Margaret	33	Marnoch	Inverkeithny	1	9
ANDREW	Mary	19	Alvah	Forglen	4	5
ANDREW	Mary	3	Marnoch	Marnoch	4	7
ANDREW	William	32	Fordyce	Forglen	4	5
ANDREW	William	53	Marnoch	Marnoch	1	6
ANDREW	William	6	Marnoch	Marnoch	4	7
ANDREW	William	4	Inverkeithny	Inverkeithny	3	13
ANGUS	Jean	45	Marnoch	Marnoch	6	23
ANGUS	John	36	Nigg KCD	Inverkeithny	1	8
ANGUS	Peter	39	Kennethmont ABD	Forglen	2	2
AUCHANACHIE	Alexander	10	Marnoch	Marnoch	6	19
AUCHANACHIE	Christian	12	Marnoch	Marnoch	6	19
AUCHANACHIE	Jean	4	Marnoch	Marnoch	6	19
AUCHANACHIE	John	50	Marnoch	Marnoch	6	19
AUCHANACHIE	Margaret	47	Turriff ABD	Marnoch	6	19
AUCHANACHIE	Peter	9	Marnoch	Marnoch	6	19
AUCHINNACHIE	Barbara	9	Marnoch	Marnoch	5	7
AUCHINNACHIE	George	3mths	Marnoch	Marnoch	5	8
AUCHINNACHIE	Isabella	7	Marnoch	Marnoch	5	8
AUCHINNACHIE	Jean	52	Marnoch	Marnoch	5	9
AUCHINNACHIE	Jean	5	Marnoch	Marnoch	5	8
AUCHINNACHIE	William	48	Marnoch	Marnoch	5	7
AUCHINNACHIE	William	11	Marnoch	Marnoch	5	7
AUCHMACHIE	Catherine	14	Marnoch	Marnoch	9	6
AUCHYMACHIE	James	11	Marnoch	Marnoch	3	17
Andrew	Jane	59	King Edward ABD	Forglen	4	5
BAGGRIE	Barbra	58	Fordyce	Marnoch	5	4
BAGREY	Margaret	62	Fordyce	Marnoch	7	14
BAGRIE	Francis	50	Turriff ABD	Marnoch	4	11
BAGRIE	Penelope	55	Turriff ABD	Marnoch	1	2
BAGRIE	Robert	28	Drumblade ABD	Inverkeithny	1	7
BAIN	Janet	45	Marnoch	Marnoch	5	12
BAIN	John	17	Rothiemay	Forglen	1	5
BAIN	William	47	Forgue ABD	Marnoch	2	6
BAIRD	Barbara	16	Forglen	Forglen	4	2
BAIRD	Christian	49	Auchterless ABD	Forglen	4	2
BAIRD	Helen	10	Forglen	Forglen	4	2
BAIRD	John	44	Monymusk ABD	Forglen	4	2
BAIRD	Mary	16	Forglen	Forglen	4	2
BALEACH	Mary	74	Fordyce	Marnoch	9	8
BALEACH	Mary	37	Marnoch	Marnoch	9	8
BALFOUR	Alexander	51	Dunfermline FIF	Forglen	2	6
BALLACH	Jane	12	Marnoch	Marnoch	7	11
BANNERMAN	Ann	74	Marnoch	Marnoch	3	3
BANNERMAN	Barbara	6	Fordyce	Marnoch	8	9
BANNERMAN	Elspet	43	Marnoch	Marnoch	6	13
BANNERMAN	George	12	Alvah	Forglen	2	7
BANNERMAN	Helen	56	Inverkeithny	Inverkeithny	2	15
BANNERMAN	Helen	17	Inverkeithny	Inverkeithny	2	7
BANNERMAN	John	82	Marnoch	Marnoch	6	13
BANZIE	Jane	14	Inverkeithny	Inverkeithny	3	14
BARBER	Ann	56	Marnoch	Forglen	4	2
BARBER	George	1	Marnoch	Marnoch	8	4
BARBER	Helen	8	Forglen	Marnoch	6	13
BARBER	Jean	17	Marnoch	Inverkeithny	3	15

SURNAME	CHR. NAME	AGE	BIRTH PLACE	CENSUS PARISH	BOOK	PG
BARBER	Jessie	9	Marnoch	Marnoch	9	9
BARBER	William	25	Marnoch	Marnoch	6	8
BARBRO	Margaret	77	Alvah	Marnoch	8	2
BARCLAY	Alexander	16	Forglen	Inverkeithny	3	2
BARCLAY	Ann	6	Gamrie	Marnoch	7	10
BARCLAY	Ann	13	Lumsden ABD	Inverkeithny	3	4
BARCLAY	George	10	Lumsden ABD	Inverkeithny	3	4
BARCLAY	Helen	9	Gamrie	Marnoch	7	9
BARCLAY	James	12	Forglen	Forglen	2	6
BARCLAY	James	42	Boyndie	Marnoch	7	9
BARCLAY	Jane	39	Forgue ABD	Inverkeithny	3	4
BARCLAY	Jane	15	Lumsden ABD	Inverkeithny	3	4
BARCLAY	Jane	7	Alvah	Marnoch	6	26
BARCLAY	Jane	8	Forgue ABD	Marnoch	5	2
BARCLAY	Jane	84	Forgue ABD	Marnoch	6	6
BARCLAY	Jane	5	Gamrie	Marnoch	7	10
BARCLAY	John	11	Gamrie	Marnoch	7	9
BARCLAY	John	16	Inverkeithny	Inverkeithny	3	1
BARCLAY	Mary	8	Gamrie	Marnoch	7	10
BARCLAY	William	40	Huntly ABD	Inverkeithny	3	4
BARCLAY	William	9	Lumsden ABD	Inverkeithny	3	5
BARNET	Jean	74	Marnoch	Marnoch	6	4
BARNETT	George	20	King Edward ABD	Inverkeithny	2	11
BARRIE	Isabella	24	Boyndie	Marnoch	4	6
BARRON	Ann	19	Udny ABD	Marnoch	7	6
BARRON	Ann	22	Marnoch	Marnoch	9	9
BARRON	George	15	Marnoch	Marnoch	6	13
BARRON	James	24	Udny ABD	Marnoch	7	6
BARRON	John	11	Marnoch	Marnoch	6	13
BARRON	Margaret	25	Udny ABD	Marnoch	7	6
BARRON	William	55	Foveran ABD	Marnoch	7	6
BARRON	William	4	Marnoch	Marnoch	7	5
BARTLETT	Henry	21	Dyce ABD	Forglen	2	7
BARTLETT	Isabella	19	Dyce ABD	Forglen	2	7
BARTLETT	James	70	Dyce ABD	Forglen	2	7
BARTLETT	Jean	67	Aboyne ABD	Forglen	2	7
BARTLETT	John	28	Dyce ABD	Forglen	2	7
BARTLETT	Margaret	23	Dyce ABD	Forglen	2	7
BARTLETT	William	25	Dyce ABD	Forglen	2	7
BATTY	Ann	1	Marnoch	Inverkeithny	3	7
BAXTER	Margaret	67	Marnoch	Marnoch	6	4
BEADIE	Anne	9	Marnoch	Marnoch	6	27
BEATIE	Robert	6	Turriff ABD	Forglen	3	6
BEATON	William	21	Boyndie	Forglen	2	2
BEATTIE	Ann	24	Auchterless ABD	Marnoch	8	3
BEATTIE	David	25	Culsalmond ABD	Marnoch	8	3
BEATTIE	George	4	Prenmay ABD	Marnoch	8	3
BEATTIE	Jean	37	Culsalmond ABD	Marnoch	6	9
BEATTIE	Jean	7	Forgue ABD	Marnoch	6	9
BEATTIE	Mary	6	Forgue ABD	Marnoch	6	9
BEATTIE	Peter	2	Forgue ABD	Marnoch	6	9
BEATTIE	William	9	Forgue ABD	Marnoch	6	9
BEDDIE	Helen	7	Marnoch	Marnoch	2	1
BEDDIE	Isabella	5	Marnoch	Marnoch	2	1
BEDDIE	James	40	Grange	Marnoch	2	1
BEDDIE	Janet	39	Banff	Marnoch	2	1
BEDDIE	Margaret	1	Marnoch	Marnoch	2	1
BEGG	Alexander	11	Forgue ABD	Marnoch	6	17
BEGG	Alexander	68	Aberdour ABD	Marnoch	5	22
BEGG	Ann	67	Rothiemay	Marnoch	4	3
BEGG	Helen	3	Forgue ABD	Marnoch	6	17
BEGG	James	6	Forgue ABD	Marnoch	6	17
BEGG	Jean	36	Marnoch	Marnoch	5	6
BEGG	John	8	Forgue ABD	Marnoch	6	17

SURNAME	CHR. NAME	AGE	BIRTH PLACE	CENSUS PARISH	BOOK	PG
BEGG	John	38	Marnoch	Marnoch	5	6
BEGG	Margaret	20	Forgue ABD	Marnoch	6	17
BEGG	Margaret	48	Forgue ABD	Marnoch	6	17
BEGG	William	54	Forgue ABD	Marnoch	6	17
BEGRIA	Alexander	62	Fordyce	Marnoch	3	7
BEGRIA	Margaret	73	Fordyce	Marnoch	3	7
BEGRIE	Christina	24	Marnoch	Marnoch	6	11
BEGRIE	Elizabeth	50	Marnoch	Marnoch	6	11
BENNET	John	9	Marnoch	Marnoch	1	2
BENNET	Lewis	16	Marnoch	Marnoch	2	8
BENNET	Margaret	40	Grange	Marnoch	1	2
BENNET	William	50	Glass ABD	Marnoch	1	2
BENNET	William	12	Marnoch	Marnoch	1	9
BENNETT	James	18	Fordyce	Marnoch	1	1
BENZIES	Alexander	81	Fordyce	Inverkeithny	1	11
BENZIES	James	37	Inverkeithny	Inverkeithny	1	10
BENZIES	James	1	Inverkeithny	Inverkeithny	1	11
BENZIES	Janet	2	Inverkeithny	Inverkeithny	1	11
BENZIES	Janet	26	Grange	Inverkeithny	1	10
BENZIES	William	4	Inverkeithny	Inverkeithny	1	11
BERRY	Alexander	8	Alford ABD	Forglen	4	3
BETTIE	Alexander	6	Forgue ABD	Marnoch	4	2
BETTIE	George	8	Forgue ABD	Marnoch	4	2
BLACK	Alexander	20	Gamrie	Forglen	2	7
BLACK	Alexander	19	Boyndie	Inverkeithny	2	9
BLACK	Christian	27	Forgue ABD	Inverkeithny	2	15
BLACK	George	32	Marnoch	Marnoch	4	2
BLACK	John	1	Marnoch	Marnoch	7	6
BLACK	Margaret	58	Marnoch	Marnoch	5	22
BLACK	William	11	Insch ABD	Marnoch	2	10
BLACK	William	27	Auchterless ABD	Inverkeithny	2	15
BLAICK	William	8	King Edward ABD	Marnoch	6	18
BLAKE	Ann	7	Marnoch	Marnoch	9	4
BOIRER?	Margaret	43	Cairnie ABD	Marnoch	5	11
BOIRIE	James	1mth	Marnoch	Marnoch	3	14
BONNER	Alexander	65	Inverurie ABD	Inverkeithny	2	13
BONNER	Alexander	11	Inverkeithny	Inverkeithny	2	13
BONNER	Elizabeth	9	Inverkeithny	Inverkeithny	2	13
BONNER	James	15	Inverurie ABD	Inverkeithny	2	13
BONNER	Jean	35	Chapel of Garioch ABD	Inverkeithny	2	13
BONNER	Margaret	13	Inverurie ABD	Inverkeithny	2	13
BONNER	William G.B.	6	Inverkeithny	Inverkeithny	2	13
BONNER	male	8mths	Inverkeithny	Inverkeithny	2	13
BONNIEMAN	Ann	23	Inverkeithny	Marnoch	4	3
BONNIEMAN	William	66	Huntly ABD	Marnoch	4	3
BONNYMAN	Alexander	12	Marnoch	Marnoch	7	14
BONNYMAN	Ann	70	Rathven	Marnoch	8	12
BONNYMAN	Eliza	1	Marnoch	Marnoch	6	24
BONNYMAN	Helen	10	Marnoch	Marnoch	6	24
BONNYMAN	Isobel	8	Marnoch	Marnoch	6	24
BONNYMAN	Jessie	6	Marnoch	Marnoch	6	24
BONNYMAN	John	4	Marnoch	Marnoch	6	24
BONNYMAN	Margaret	35	Marnoch	Marnoch	6	24
BONNYMAN	Walter	40	Gamrie	Marnoch	6	24
BONNYMAN	William	13	Fordyce	Marnoch	6	24
BONNYMAN	helen	17	Glass ABD	Marnoch	2	4
BONNYMANN	William	20	Inverkeithny	Marnoch	8	5
BOOTH	George	4	Forglen	Forglen	3	4
BOOTH	George	12	Marnoch	Marnoch	3	9
BOOTH	Lilly	46	Marnoch	Marnoch	9	9
BOOTH	Margaret	72	Pluscarden MOR	Marnoch	1	1
BOOTH	William	71	Chapel of Garioch ABD	Marnoch	1	1
BOURIE	Alexander	6	Marnoch	Marnoch	1	5
BOURIE	Isobel	15	Marnoch	Marnoch	1	5

SURNAME	CHR. NAME	AGE	BIRTH PLACE	CENSUS PARISH	BOOK	PG
BOURIE	James	50	Huntly ABD	Marnoch	1	5
BOURIE	Jessie	11	Marnoch	Marnoch	1	5
BOURIE	Margaret	9	Marnoch	Marnoch	1	5
BOURIE	Margaret	46	Forgue ABD	Marnoch	1	5
BOWIE	Eliza	15	Marnoch	Marnoch	4	10
BOWIE	Elizabeth	10	Drumblade ABD	Marnoch	2	1
BOWIE	Isabella	12	Drumblade ABD	Marnoch	2	1
BOWIE	Isabella	48	Mortlach	Marnoch	2	1
BOWIE	James	4	Marnoch	Marnoch	2	1
BOWIE	Jane	8	Marnoch	Marnoch	2	1
BOWIE	John	14	Drumblade ABD	Marnoch	2	2
BOWIE	John	49	Huntly ABD	Marnoch	2	1
BOWIE	John	12	Marnoch	Marnoch	4	10
BOYNE	Jane	86	Marnoch	Marnoch	7	3
BRACKIE	Catherine	22	Marnoch	Marnoch	8	7
BRACKIE	Catherine	80	New Deer ABD	Marnoch	8	7
BRACKIE	William	11	Marnoch	Marnoch	8	7
BRANDER	Andrew	18	Ordiquhill	Marnoch	8	5
BRANDERS	John	10	Marnoch	Marnoch	7	13
BRANDERS	Robert	14	Ordiquhill	Marnoch	7	14
BRANDIE	Helen	1	Marnoch	Marnoch	5	23
BRANDIE	William	3	Inverkeithny	Marnoch	5	23
BRANDS	Anne	1	Boyndie	Marnoch	3	4
BRANDS	Elizabeth	3	Marnoch	Marnoch	3	4
BRANDS	Margaret	25	King Edward ABD	Marnoch	3	4
BREMNER	Alexander	3mths	Inverkeithny	Inverkeithny	3	13
BREMNER	Alexander	56	Marnoch	Marnoch	4	14
BREMNER	Alexander	11	Marnoch	Marnoch	4	14
BREMNER	Barbara	26	Marnoch	Marnoch	6	10
BREMNER	Catherine	7	Marnoch	Marnoch	7	3
BREMNER	Christian	47	Auchterless ABD	Marnoch	7	3
BREMNER	Christian	18	Marnoch	Marnoch	4	14
BREMNER	Elizabeth	50	Banff	Forglen	4	9
BREMNER	Elizabeth	35	Marnoch	Marnoch	1	10
BREMNER	Elizabeth	53	King Edward ABD	Marnoch	1	7
BREMNER	Elsie	1	Marnoch	Marnoch	6	10
BREMNER	Elspet	15	Marnoch	Marnoch	4	13
BREMNER	Elspet	51	Insch ABD	Marnoch	4	14
BREMNER	George	56	Marnoch	Marnoch	4	10
BREMNER	George	9	Inverkeithny	Inverkeithny	3	13
BREMNER	George	51	Marnoch	Marnoch	7	3
BREMNER	George	45	Rothiemay	Marnoch	1	7
BREMNER	Harriet	19	Cairnie ABD	Marnoch	9	2
BREMNER	Helen	77	Rothiemay	Marnoch	1	9
BREMNER	Isabella	60	Boyndie	Marnoch	4	11
BREMNER	Isobel	21	Marnoch	Marnoch	4	14
BREMNER	James	43	Marnoch	Marnoch	6	10
BREMNER	James	10	Inverkeithny	Inverkeithny	3	13
BREMNER	James	37	Grange	Forglen	4	9
BREMNER	James	19	Marnoch	Marnoch	7	3
BREMNER	Jane	20	Cairnie ABD	Marnoch	3	9
BREMNER	Jane	1mth	Marnoch	Marnoch	6	11
BREMNER	Jane	4	Inverkeithny	Inverkeithny	3	13
BREMNER	Jane	39	Marnoch	Inverkeithny	3	13
BREMNER	Janet	13	Marnoch	Marnoch	4	14
BREMNER	John	47	Marnoch	Marnoch	7	3
BREMNER	John	18	Marnoch	Marnoch	5	19
BREMNER	John	6	Inverkeithny	Inverkeithny	3	13
BREMNER	John	69	Marnoch	Marnoch	3	9
BREMNER	Margaret	70	Marnoch	Marnoch	4	14
BREMNER	Margaret	51	Crimond ABD	Marnoch	5	19
BREMNER	Margaret	24	Marnoch	Marnoch	7	3
BREMNER	Margaret	39	Rothiemay	Marnoch	1	10
BREMNER	Margaret	70	Marnoch	Marnoch	3	9

SURNAME	CHR. NAME	AGE	BIRTH PLACE	CENSUS PARISH	BOOK	PG
BREMNER	Mary	30	Marnoch	Marnoch	3	9
BREMNER	Mary	13	Marnoch	Marnoch	5	19
BREMNER	Mary	19	Banff	Forglen	4	9
BREMNER	Peter	9	Marnoch	Marnoch	7	3
BREMNER	Robert	44	Marnoch	Inverkeithny	3	13
BREMNER	Robert	2	Inverkeithny	Inverkeithny	3	13
BREMNER	William	36	Rothiemay	Marnoch	1	9
BREMNER	William	17	Fyvie ABD	Marnoch	9	8
BREMNER	William	6	Marnoch	Marnoch	5	26
BREMNER	William	53	Marnoch	Marnoch	7	3
BREMNER	William	11	Marnoch	Marnoch	7	3
BROCKIE	Charles	20	Marnoch	Marnoch	8	3
BROCKIE	Elizabeth	24	Marnoch	Marnoch	8	8
BRODIE	Alexander	35	-	Marnoch	4	6
BRODIE	Alexander	66	Ordiquhill	Forglen	1	7
BRODIE	Ann	32	Forglen	Marnoch	9	10
BRODIE	Ann	58	Grange	Marnoch	5	8
BRODIE	Elizabeth	19	Rothiemay	Inverkeithny	3	12
BRODIE	Helen	21	Marnoch	Marnoch	6	22
BRODIE	Helen	73	Marnoch	Marnoch	4	6
BRODIE	Helen	64	Marnoch	Marnoch	5	19
BRODIE	Isabella	64	Cullen	Forglen	1	7
BRODIE	Jessie	23	Forglen	Forglen	1	7
BRODIE	William	17	Marnoch	Marnoch	6	22
BRODIE	William	50	Marnoch	Marnoch	6	22
BROWN	Agnes	40	Cairnie ABD	Marnoch	1	11
BROWN	Ann	39	Fraserburgh ABD	Forglen	3	6
BROWN	Catherine J.A.	3	Marnoch	Marnoch	3	11
BROWN	Christian	44	Marnoch	Marnoch	5	16
BROWN	David	2	Marnoch	Marnoch	5	1
BROWN	George	29	Alvah	Forglen	2	9
BROWN	George	57	Prenmay ABD	Marnoch	1	11
BROWN	George	13	Culsalmond ABD	Marnoch	1	11
BROWN	George W.	4	Forglen	Forglen	3	6
BROWN	Gilbert	33	Turriff ABD	Forglen	3	6
BROWN	Gilbert	9	New Pitsligo ABD	Forglen	3	6
BROWN	Helen	11	Drummond ROC	Marnoch	6	19
BROWN	James	10	Marnoch	Marnoch	5	1
BROWN	James	18	Culsalmond ABD	Marnoch	4	9
BROWN	James	44	Botriphnie	Forglen	3	1
BROWN	Jane	39	Marnoch	Marnoch	5	1
BROWN	Jane	11	Ordiquhill	Marnoch	2	1
BROWN	John	39	Marnoch	Marnoch	5	1
BROWN	John	-	-	Marnoch	8	6
BROWN	John	10	Culsalmond ABD	Marnoch	1	11
BROWN	John	31	Culsalmond ABD	Marnoch	9	7
BROWN	John	18	Marnoch	Marnoch	5	1
BROWN	John A.	9	Marnoch	Marnoch	3	11
BROWN	Margaret	12	Marnoch	Marnoch	5	1
BROWN	Margaret	22	Gamrie	Inverkeithny	2	8
BROWN	Mary	8	Marnoch	Marnoch	5	1
BROWN	Mary	27	Marnoch	Marnoch	6	3
BROWN	Rachel	29	Boyndie	Marnoch	3	11
BROWN	Robert	6	Marnoch	Marnoch	5	1
BROWN	William	46	Boyndie	Marnoch	3	11
BROWN	William	7	Forglen	Forglen	3	6
BROWN	William A.	6	Marnoch	Marnoch	3	11
BRUCE	Alexander	46	Forgue ABD	Forglen	3	5
BRUCE	Alexander	20	Strichen ABD	Inverkeithny	1	10
BRUCE	Ann	31	Leslie ABD	Forglen	3	5
BRUCE	Ann	60	Auchterless ABD	Marnoch	4	4
BRUCE	Anne	30	Gamrie	Marnoch	6	6
BRUCE	Isabella	1	Forglen	Forglen	3	5
BRUCE	James	32	Grange	Marnoch	2	8

SURNAME	CHR. NAME	AGE	BIRTH PLACE	CENSUS PARISH	BOOK	PG
BRUCE	Jessie	40	Banff	Marnoch	3	13
BRUCE	Margaret	30	Marnoch	Marnoch	2	8
BRUCE	Robert	30	Aberdeen ABD	Marnoch	4	4
BUCHAN	Agnes	25	Forgue ABD	Inverkeithny	3	4
BUCHAN	Agnes	16	Forglen	Marnoch	8	10
BUCHAN	Alexander	20	Forgue ABD	Forglen	4	1
BUCHAN	Ann	16	Forgue ABD	Marnoch	8	10
BUCHAN	Elizabeth	57	Auchterless ABD	Forglen	3	4
BUCHAN	Elsie	49	Aberdeen ABD	Marnoch	8	11
BUCHAN	George	57	Forglen	Forglen	3	4
BUCHAN	Isabel	18	Forgue ABD	Inverkeithny	3	4
BUCHAN	James	71	Forgue ABD	Marnoch	5	21
BUCHAN	Jessie	24	Forglen	Marnoch	8	11
BUCHAN	John	48	Forglen	Marnoch	8	11
BUCHAN	Margaret	10	Forglen	Marnoch	8	11
BUCHAN	William	7	Forglen	Marnoch	8	11
BUCHAN	William	21	Forglen	Forglen	3	4
BUCHAN	William	5	Inverkeithny	Inverkeithny	3	14
BUIE	Lewis	73	Cairnie ABD	Marnoch	2	8
BUIE	Margaret	78	Grange	Marnoch	2	8
CALDER	Leslie	21	Rathven	Marnoch	1	14
CALLUM	Alexander	12	Kildrummy ABD	Marnoch	1	4
CALLUM	Celia	4	Marnoch	Marnoch	1	4
CALLUM	Christian	37	Kildrummy ABD	Marnoch	1	4
CALLUM	David	1	Marnoch	Marnoch	1	4
CALLUM	John	6	Auchindoir ABD	Marnoch	1	4
CALLUM	John	34	Strathdon ABD	Marnoch	1	4
CALLUm	Margaret	9	Kildrummy ABD	Marnoch	1	4
CAMERON	Annie	55	Banff	Marnoch	6	17
CAMERON	Isabella	20	Arbuthnott KCD	Inverkeithny	2	3
CAMPBELL	James	23	Ireland	Inverkeithny	1	2
CAMPBELL	James	24	Courn? MOG IRL	Inverkeithny	1	3
CAMPBELL	Margaret	26	Aberdeen ABD	Marnoch	2	13
CARD	Margaret	85	Forglen	Forglen	1	1
CARNEGIE	Alexander	9	Forglen	Forglen	1	6
CARNEGIE	David	13	Forglen	Forglen	1	6
CARNEGIE	James	58	Bervie KCD	Forglen	1	5
CARNEGIE	Jane	20	Forglen	Forglen	1	5
CARNEGIE	Janet	57	Forgue ABD	Forglen	1	5
CARNEGIE	John	17	Forglen	Forglen	1	6
CARNEGIE	Margaret	15	Forglen	Forglen	1	6
CARNEGIE	Mary	11	Forglen	Forglen	1	6
CAY	Alexander	17	Midmar ABD	Marnoch	4	13
CENTRE	Isabella	48	Marnoch	Marnoch	8	7
CHALMERS	Alexander	2	Marnoch	Marnoch	5	25
CHALMERS	Elspet	50	Deskford	Marnoch	6	11
CHALMERS	George	80	Forgue ABD	Forglen	4	1
CHALMERS	Isabella	50	King Edward ABD	Marnoch	5	21
CHALMERS	Janet	41	Deskford	Marnoch	6	15
CHALMERS	Jean	22	Marnoch	Marnoch	6	24
CHALMERS	Joseph	16	Marnoch	Marnoch	6	24
CHALMERS	Margaret	15	Marnoch	Marnoch	6	29
CHALMERS	Mary	35	Forgue ABD	Forglen	4	1
CHALMERS	Susan	74	Forgue ABD	Forglen	4	1
CHAPMAN	Mary	22	Auchterless ABD	Inverkeithny	3	9
CHARLES	Elizabeth	80	Monquhitter ABD	Marnoch	5	12
CHEYNE	Jean	74	Marnoch	Marnoch	5	9
CHISHOLM	Alexander	12	Marnoch	Marnoch	6	23
CHISHOLM	Eliza	19	Marnoch	Marnoch	6	23
CHISHOLM	James	46	Boyndie	Inverkeithny	3	13
CHISHOLM	James	17	Boyndie	Marnoch	5	21
CHISHOLM	James	19	Fordyce	Marnoch	8	5
CHISHOLM	Jane	14	Marnoch	Marnoch	6	23
CHISHOLM	Jean	46	Alvah	Marnoch	6	23

SURNAME	CHR. NAME	AGE	BIRTH PLACE	CENSUS PARISH	BOOK	PG
CHISHOLM	John	20	Ordiquhill	Marnoch	9	2
CHISHOLM	William	10	Marnoch	Marnoch	6	23
CHISHOLM	William	47	Nairn NAI	Marnoch	6	23
CHISOM	Mary	45	Banff	Marnoch	7	4
CHISOM	Walter	14	Ordiquhill	Marnoch	7	4
CHISOM	William	12	Ordiquhill	Marnoch	7	4
CHIVAS	Andrew	62	King Edward ABD	Marnoch	6	10
CHIVAS	Jean	25	Forgue ABD	Marnoch	6	10
CHRISTIE	Alexander	47	King Edward ABD	Marnoch	4	12
CHRISTIE	Alexander	13	Monquhitter ABD	Marnoch	4	12
CHRISTIE	Ann	32	Inverkeithny	Marnoch	6	2
CHRISTIE	Barbra	8	Marnoch	Marnoch	1	3
CHRISTIE	Christian	10	Marnoch	Marnoch	1	3
CHRISTIE	David	5	Turriff ABD	Marnoch	4	6
CHRISTIE	Elizabeth	4	Turriff ABD	Marnoch	4	6
CHRISTIE	Elspet	43	Marnoch	Marnoch	4	15
CHRISTIE	George	45	Alvah	Marnoch	6	6
CHRISTIE	George	50	Marnoch	Marnoch	4	15
CHRISTIE	Helen	2	Forglen	Marnoch	6	9
CHRISTIE	Helen	36	Gamrie	Marnoch	7	9
CHRISTIE	Helen	10mths	Marnoch	Marnoch	6	2
CHRISTIE	Isabella	22	Banff	Marnoch	8	5
CHRISTIE	Isabella	36	Old Deer ABD	Marnoch	4	6
CHRISTIE	Isabella	4	Marnoch	Marnoch	6	2
CHRISTIE	Isabella	48	Fordyce	Marnoch	4	12
CHRISTIE	Isabella M.	4mths	Marnoch	Marnoch	4	6
CHRISTIE	Isobel	50	Longside ABD	Marnoch	1	3
CHRISTIE	Isobel	5	Marnoch	Marnoch	1	3
CHRISTIE	James	6	Marnoch	Marnoch	6	2
CHRISTIE	James	34	Ordiquhill	Marnoch	9	8
CHRISTIE	James	14	Marnoch	Marnoch	1	3
CHRISTIE	James	31	Gartly ABD	Marnoch	9	8
CHRISTIE	James	58	Forgue ABD	Marnoch	1	3
CHRISTIE	Jane	33	Boyndie	Forglen	4	3
CHRISTIE	Jane	50	Marnoch	Marnoch	6	6
CHRISTIE	Janet	26	Forglen	Marnoch	6	9
CHRISTIE	Janet	94	Marnoch	Marnoch	6	11
CHRISTIE	Janet	50	Marnoch	Marnoch	6	16
CHRISTIE	Jean	11	Monquhitter ABD	Marnoch	4	12
CHRISTIE	Jean	2	Marnoch	Marnoch	4	6
CHRISTIE	John	9	Auchindoir ABD	Inverkeithny	3	7
CHRISTIE	John	8	Turriff ABD	Marnoch	4	6
CHRISTIE	John	18	Boyndie	Marnoch	8	12
CHRISTIE	John	46	Alvah	Marnoch	4	6
CHRISTIE	Joseph	24	Banff	Marnoch	6	9
CHRISTIE	Margaret	28	Midmar ABD	Inverkeithny	3	7
CHRISTIE	Margaret	6	Auchindoir ABD	Inverkeithny	3	7
CHRISTIE	Margaret	3	Forglen	Marnoch	6	9
CHRISTIE	Mary	38	Glass ABD	Marnoch	2	4
CHRISTIE	Rachel	27	Forglen	Marnoch	6	23
CHRISTIE	Thomas	40	Ordiquhill	Marnoch	2	4
CHRISTIE	William	15	Monquhitter ABD	Marnoch	4	12
CHRISTIE	William	46	Keith	Marnoch	9	8
CHRISTIE	William	26	Kildrummy ABD	Marnoch	3	18
CHYNE	Jean	68	Marnoch	Marnoch	5	2
CLARK	Agnes	24	Marnoch	Marnoch	8	11
CLARK	Alexander	16	Gamrie	Forglen	4	4
CLARK	Alexander	68	Forglen	Marnoch	5	19
CLARK	Alexander	13	Marnoch	Marnoch	6	20
CLARK	Alexander	71	Marnoch	Marnoch	8	11
CLARK	Alexander	8	Ordiquhill	Marnoch	8	11
CLARK	Ann	58	Inverkeithny	Inverkeithny	1	1
CLARK	Ann	57	Marnoch	Marnoch	2	7
CLARK	Ann	3	Marnoch	Marnoch	8	11

SURNAME	CHR. NAME	AGE	BIRTH PLACE	CENSUS PARISH	BOOK	PG
CLARK	Ann	72	Fordyce	Marnoch	8	11
CLARK	Anne	29	Monquhitter ABD	Marnoch	6	8
CLARK	Barbara	17	Auchterless ABD	Marnoch	8	7
CLARK	Catherine	82	Marnoch	Inverkeithny	1	8
CLARK	Catherine	34	Auchterless ABD	Marnoch	4	2
CLARK	Christian	42	Inverkeithny	Inverkeithny	1	8
CLARK	Elizabeth	59	Inverkeithny	Inverkeithny	2	18
CLARK	George	15	Forgue ABD	Marnoch	1	10
CLARK	George	8	Forgue ABD	Marnoch	6	21
CLARK	Helen	15	Rathven	Forglen	1	3
CLARK	Helen	5	Marnoch	Marnoch	6	21
CLARK	Helen	24	Tough ABD	Marnoch	5	17
CLARK	Helen	6	Marnoch	Marnoch	8	11
CLARK	Helen	5	Marnoch	Marnoch	5	19
CLARK	Helen	30	King Edward ABD	Marnoch	5	19
CLARK	Helen	36	Ordiquhill	Marnoch	8	11
CLARK	Isabella	17	Marnoch	Marnoch	2	7
CLARK	James	2mths	Marnoch	Marnoch	6	21
CLARK	James	75	Marnoch	Marnoch	6	25
CLARK	Jane	78	Marnoch	Marnoch	6	25
CLARK	Jane	31	King Edward ABD	Marnoch	6	20
CLARK	Jean	30	Tough ABD	Marnoch	5	16
CLARK	Jean	2	Marnoch	Marnoch	6	5
CLARK	John	26	Marnoch	Marnoch	2	7
CLARK	John	46	Marnoch	Marnoch	5	19
CLARK	John	69	Rathven	Marnoch	2	7
CLARK	Joseph	9	Monquhitter ABD	Marnoch	6	8
CLARK	Margaret	32	Marnoch	Marnoch	2	5
CLARK	Mary	9	Inverkeithny	Inverkeithny	2	6
CLARK	Mary	32	Marnoch	Marnoch	6	23
CLARK	Robert	2mths	Marnoch	Marnoch	8	11
CLARK	Susan	25	Auchterless ABD	Marnoch	1	1
CLARK	Thomas	34	Marnoch	Marnoch	8	11
CLARK	William	29	Tough ABD	Marnoch	5	16
CLARK	William	34	Marnoch	Marnoch	6	20
CLARK	William	38	Marnoch	Marnoch	4	2
CLARK	William	11	Inverkeithny	Marnoch	6	21
CLARK	William	69	Daviot INV	Marnoch	5	16
CLARK	William	13	Forglen	Marnoch	3	18
COBBAN	Alexander	25	Forgue ABD	Inverkeithny	2	12
COCKBURN	Alexander	26	Stenton,Haddington	Marnoch	2	5
COCKBURN	Isabel	24	Forgue ABD	Inverkeithny	2	13
COLLIE	Jane	7	Marnoch	Marnoch	8	3
COLLINS	Daniel	44	Ireland	Marnoch	5	16
COLLINS	John	29	Melrose ROX	Inverkeithny	1	12
CONN	Alexander	40	Forgue ABD	Marnoch	6	28
CONN	Alexander	7mths	Marnoch	Marnoch	6	5
CONN	Catherine	7	Forgue ABD	Marnoch	6	5
CONN	Catherine	77	Marnoch	Marnoch	6	28
CONN	Elspet	27	Forgue ABD	Marnoch	6	5
CONN	Helen	5	Forglen	Marnoch	6	5
CONN	Lillias	16	Marnoch	Marnoch	9	1
COOK	John	32	Rhynie ABD	Marnoch	1	10
COOK	Mary	24	Insch ABD	Marnoch	1	10
COOK	Mary Ann	2	Clatt ABD	Marnoch	1	10
COOPER	Agnes	31	King Edward ABD	Marnoch	6	18
COOPER	Alexander	21	Boyndie	Forglen	2	2
COOPER	George	23	Forgue ABD	Marnoch	6	18
COOPER	George	59	Forgue ABD	Marnoch	4	2
COOPER	James	18	Forgue ABD	Marnoch	4	2
COOPER	Margaret	6	Marnoch	Marnoch	4	2
COOPER	Margaret	3	Marnoch	Marnoch	6	18
COOPER	Margaret	56	Forgue ABD	Marnoch	4	2
COOPER	Mary A.	1	Marnoch	Marnoch	6	12

SURNAME	CHR. NAME	AGE	BIRTH PLACE	CENSUS PARISH	BOOK	PG
COOPER	jean	21	Forgue ABD	Marnoch	4	2
COPLAND	Ann	27	Inverkeithny	Inverkeithny	2	5
COPLAND	Elizabeth	50	Marnoch	Inverkeithny	2	5
COPLAND	George	21	Ordiquhill	Marnoch	3	16
COPLAND	Helen	19	Inverkeithny	Marnoch	8	3
COPLAND	Helen	58	Marnoch	Marnoch	3	16
COPLAND	Henrietta	31	Inverkeithny	Inverkeithny	2	5
COPLAND	Isabella	11	Inverkeithny	Inverkeithny	2	5
COPLAND	Jane	11	Rathven	Marnoch	3	16
COPLAND	Jessie	14	Inverkeithny	Marnoch	4	7
COPLAND	Mary	5	Inverkeithny	Inverkeithny	2	5
COPLAND	William	9	Inverkeithny	Inverkeithny	2	5
COPLAND	William	70	Huntly ABD	Marnoch	3	16
COPLAND	george	5	Marnoch	Marnoch	4	2
CORMACK	George	31	Rothiemay	Marnoch	5	8
CORMACK	Robert	17	Huntly ABD	Forglen	1	7
CORMACK	Robert	14	Drumblade ABD	Marnoch	9	4
COULL	Alexander	1	Marnoch	Marnoch	9	3
COULL	Elspet	34	Huntly ABD	Marnoch	9	3
COULL	John	4	Marnoch	Marnoch	9	3
COULL	John	33	Rathven	Marnoch	9	3
COULL	Margaret	9	Marnoch	Marnoch	9	3
COULL	Margaret	15	Rathven	Marnoch	3	9
COULL	Willam	7	Marnoch	Marnoch	9	3
COURAGE	Isabel	42	Marnoch	Marnoch	5	20
COURAGE	James	44	Marnoch	Marnoch	5	20
COUTTS	Charles	31	Crathie ABD	Inverkeithny	3	14
COUTTS	John	42	Crathie ABD	Inverkeithny	3	14
COUTTS	John	14	Auchterless ABD	Inverkeithny	3	14
COW	Harry	57	Auchindoir ABD	Inverkeithny	2	5
COW	James	38	Gartly ABD	Inverkeithny	2	5
COW	Margaret	38	Alford ABD	Marnoch	5	7
COWE	Catherine	61	Marnoch	Marnoch	6	26
COWE	James	61	Marnoch	Marnoch	6	26
COWE	William	12	Marnoch	Marnoch	1	3
COWE	William	22	Marnoch	Marnoch	6	26
COWIE	Agnes	25	Turriff ABD	Inverkeithny	2	17
COWIE	Alexander	17	Marnoch	Inverkeithny	3	5
COWIE	Ann	66	Fordyce	Forglen	4	9
COWIE	Ann	52	Inverkeithny	Inverkeithny	2	17
COWIE	Ann	34	Ordiquhill	Forglen	4	9
COWIE	Ann	9	Inverkeithny	Inverkeithny	2	17
COWIE	Ann	16	Marnoch	Marnoch	6	14
COWIE	Barbara	12	Inverkeithny	Inverkeithny	2	17
COWIE	Catherine	5	Marnoch	Marnoch	7	4
COWIE	Christina	28	Logie Buchan ABD	Inverkeithny	3	6
COWIE	Elspet	31	Inveravon	Marnoch	7	4
COWIE	George	30	Forgue ABD	Inverkeithny	3	5
COWIE	Helen	14	Inverkeithny	Inverkeithny	3	10
COWIE	James	3	Forgue ABD	Inverkeithny	3	5
COWIE	James	66	Ordiquhill	Forglen	4	9
COWIE	James	21	Marnoch	Inverkeithny	3	4
COWIE	James	20	Culsalmond ABD	Inverkeithny	3	1
COWIE	James	65	England	Marnoch	3	7
COWIE	John	50	Inverkeithny	Inverkeithny	2	17
COWIE	John	25	Inverkeithny	Inverkeithny	2	17
COWIE	John	19	Marnoch	Inverkeithny	2	13
COWIE	John	31	Ordiquhill	Marnoch	7	4
COWIE	John	3	Marnoch	Marnoch	7	4
COWIE	Magdalene	17	Inverkeithny	Inverkeithny	3	6
COWIE	Mary	17	Marnoch	Marnoch	6	26
COWIE	Mary	3mths	Marnoch	Marnoch	7	5
COWIE	William	1	Inverkeithny	Inverkeithny	2	17
COWIE	William	16	Marnoch	Marnoch	8	10

SURNAME	CHR. NAME	AGE	BIRTH PLACE	CENSUS PARISH	BOOK	PG
CRAIB	Alexander	80	Marnoch	Marnoch	8	12
CRAIB	Charles	20	King Edward ABD	Marnoch	8	9
CRAIB	George	43	Inverkeithny	Marnoch	8	12
CRAIB	Jessie	20	Forglen	Marnoch	8	12
CRAIB	Margaret	80	Marnoch	Marnoch	8	12
CRAIG	Alexander	2	Marnoch	Marnoch	6	24
CRAIG	Alexander	69	Ordiquhill	Marnoch	3	10
CRAIG	John	17	Alvah	Forglen	1	7
CRAIGENS	Barbara	23	Marnoch	Inverkeithny	1	10
CRAIGENS	James	50	Inverkeithny	Inverkeithny	1	10
CRAIGENS	Mary Ann	1	Inverkeithny	Inverkeithny	1	10
CRAIGENS	William	11	Inverkeithny	Marnoch	3	18
CRAN	Alexander	73	Marnoch	Marnoch	7	5
CRAN	Elizabeth	28	Marnoch	Inverkeithny	3	12
CRAN	George	6	Inverkeithny	Inverkeithny	3	12
CRAN	Helen	9	Inverkeithny	Inverkeithny	1	5
CRAN	Helen	35	Inverkeithny	Inverkeithny	1	5
CRAN	Helen	36	Marnoch	Marnoch	7	5
CRAN	Helen	60	Marnoch	Marnoch	7	5
CRAN	Isabella	1	Inverkeithny	Inverkeithny	1	11
CRAN	Isabella	7	Inverkeithny	Inverkeithny	1	5
CRAN	Isabella	33	Marnoch	Marnoch	6	19
CRAN	James	1	Inverkeithny	Inverkeithny	1	6
CRAN	James	33	Forgue ABD	Inverkeithny	1	5
CRAN	Jean	73	New Deer ABD	Inverkeithny	1	9
CRAN	Jean	3	Inverkeithny	Inverkeithny	1	5
CRAN	John	19	Inverkeithny	Inverkeithny	1	6
CRAN	Margaret	72	Marnoch	Inverkeithny	1	9
CRAN	Margaret	9	Inverkeithny	Inverkeithny	1	9
CRAN	Margaret	3	Inverkeithny	Inverkeithny	1	7
CRAN	Mary	28	Auchterless ABD	Inverkeithny	1	7
CRAN	Peter	5	Inverkeithny	Inverkeithny	1	5
CRAN	Peter	36	Inverkeithny	Inverkeithny	1	7
CRAN	Robert	72	Inverkeithny	Inverkeithny	1	9
CRAN	William	1	Inverkeithny	Inverkeithny	1	7
CRANN	Elizabeth	76	Marnoch	Marnoch	6	14
CRAWFORD	George	10mths	Marnoch	Marnoch	5	2
CRAWFORD	James	40	Crathie ABD	Marnoch	4	13
CRAWFORD	William	24	Turriff ABD	Forglen	2	9
CRICHTON	John	22	Methlick ABD	Inverkeithny	3	10
CRUICKSHANK	Alexander	3	Inverkeithny	Inverkeithny	3	7
CRUICKSHANK	Alexander	54	Botriphnie	Marnoch	2	5
CRUICKSHANK	Alexander	3	Forglen	Marnoch	4	4
CRUICKSHANK	Ann	15	Marnoch	Inverkeithny	3	7
CRUICKSHANK	Ann	4mths	Marnoch	Marnoch	4	4
CRUICKSHANK	Barbara	5	Forglen	Marnoch	4	4
CRUICKSHANK	Catherine	30	Marnoch	Marnoch	7	6
CRUICKSHANK	Charles	6mths	Marnoch	Marnoch	1	3
CRUICKSHANK	Eliza	22	Forgue ABD	Marnoch	8	1
CRUICKSHANK	Elspet	36	Banff	Marnoch	4	4
CRUICKSHANK	George	35	Alvah	Inverkeithny	3	7
CRUICKSHANK	George	16	Boyndie	Marnoch	8	6
CRUICKSHANK	George	7	Forglen	Marnoch	4	4
CRUICKSHANK	George	14	Marnoch	Marnoch	7	4
CRUICKSHANK	Helen	48	Rothiemay	Inverkeithny	3	11
CRUICKSHANK	Helen	12	Inverkeithny	Inverkeithny	3	8
CRUICKSHANK	Isabel	25	Ordiquhill	Forglen	1	1
CRUICKSHANK	Isabella	27	Forglen	Marnoch	5	24
CRUICKSHANK	Isabella	19	Turriff ABD	Marnoch	4	10
CRUICKSHANK	James	39	Inverkeithny	Forglen	2	9
CRUICKSHANK	James	6	Inverkeithny	Inverkeithny	3	7
CRUICKSHANK	James	49	Forgue ABD	Inverkeithny	3	9
CRUICKSHANK	James	4	Marnoch	Marnoch	1	3
CRUICKSHANK	James	35	Rayne ABD	Marnoch	8	6

SURNAME	CHR. NAME	AGE	BIRTH PLACE	CENSUS PARISH	BOOK	PG
CRUICKSHANK	James	10	Forglen	Marnoch	4	4
CRUICKSHANK	Jane	1	Marnoch	Marnoch	5	24
CRUICKSHANK	Janet	50	Aberlour	Marnoch	2	5
CRUICKSHANK	Janet	10	Botriphnie	Marnoch	2	5
CRUICKSHANK	Janet	7	Forgue ABD	Marnoch	1	3
CRUICKSHANK	Janet	30	Marnoch	Marnoch	1	3
CRUICKSHANK	Jean	11	Marnoch	Marnoch	4	4
CRUICKSHANK	Jessie G.	21	Inverkeithny	Inverkeithny	3	9
CRUICKSHANK	John	18	Marnoch	Forglen	3	5
CRUICKSHANK	John	14	Rothiemay	Marnoch	4	7
CRUICKSHANK	John	9	Forglen	Marnoch	4	4
CRUICKSHANK	John	3	Forgue ABD	Marnoch	5	24
CRUICKSHANK	John	10mths	Marnoch	Marnoch	3	12
CRUICKSHANK	Katherine	47	Marnoch	Marnoch	5	15
CRUICKSHANK	Margaret	39	Auchterless ABD	Inverkeithny	3	7
CRUICKSHANK	Margaret	8	Botriphnie	Marnoch	2	5
CRUICKSHANK	Margaret B.	1	Inverkeithny	Inverkeithny	3	9
CRUICKSHANK	Mary	19	Forgue ABD	Inverkeithny	3	13
CRUICKSHANK	Mary	35	Inverkeithny	Inverkeithny	3	7
CRUICKSHANK	Mary	50	Forglen	Marnoch	7	4
CRUICKSHANK	Penelope	45	Gamrie	Inverkeithny	3	9
CRUICKSHANK	Robert	11	Forgue ABD	Forglen	3	4
CRUICKSHANK	William	46	Turriff ABD	Inverkeithny	3	11
CRUICKSHANK	William	10	Inverkeithny	Inverkeithny	3	7
CRUICKSHANK	William	27	Marnoch	Marnoch	7	3
CRUICKSHANK	William	34	Rayne ABD	Marnoch	4	4
CRUICKSHANKS	Amelia	81	Marnoch	Marnoch	6	29
CUMMING	Elizabeth	67	Alvah	Marnoch	6	27
CUMMING	Elspet	6	Forglen	Forglen	2	3
CUMMING	George	58	Marnoch	Marnoch	6	27
CUMMING	Grace	33	Auchterless ABD	Marnoch	3	9
CUMMING	Helen	17	Marnoch	Marnoch	5	26
CUMMING	Helen	53	Alvah	Marnoch	5	26
CUMMING	Isabella	24	Abernethy INV	Inverkeithny	2	12
CUMMING	Jean	15	Turriff ABD	Forglen	2	3
CUMMING	Jean	49	Monquhitter ABD	Forglen	2	3
CUMMING	Joseph	12	Forglen	Forglen	2	3
CUMMING	Margaret	52	Rothes MOR	Marnoch	3	8
CUMMING	Mary	10	Forglen	Forglen	2	3
CUMMING	Mary	58	Alvah	Marnoch	6	27
CUMMING	Mary	13	Marnoch	Marnoch	5	26
CUMMING	Walter	23	Fearn ROC	Inverkeithny	2	6
CUMMING	William	61	Marnoch	Marnoch	5	26
CURRIE	Ann	26	Marnoch	Marnoch	4	8
CURRIE	Isabella	30	Marnoch	Marnoch	4	8
CURRIE	Janet	49	Marnoch	Marnoch	4	8
CURRIE	William	28	Marnoch	Marnoch	4	8
CURRIE	William	59	Grange	Marnoch	4	8
CUTHBERT	Alexander	16	King Edward ABD	Marnoch	5	24
CUTHBERT	James	61	Keith	Marnoch	5	24
CUTHBERT	James	20	Turriff ABD	Marnoch	5	24
Cone	Jean	73	Banff	Forglen	2	5
Craib	Charles	1	Marnoch	Marnoch	8	9
DALLAS	George	4	Marnoch	Marnoch	5	17
DALLAS	George	39	Gamrie	Marnoch	5	17
DALLAS	Isabella	40	King Edward ABD	Marnoch	5	17
DALLAS	Isabella	2	Marnoch	Marnoch	5	17
DALLAS	James	9	Marnoch	Marnoch	5	17
DALLAS	Jean	1	Marnoch	Marnoch	5	17
DALLAS	Margaret	7	Marnoch	Marnoch	5	17
DALLAS	Mary	6	Marnoch	Marnoch	5	17
DAVIDSON	Alexander	3	Marnoch	Marnoch	7	2
DAVIDSON	Ann	6	Marnoch	Marnoch	7	1
DAVIDSON	Barbara	36	Longside ABD	Marnoch	7	1

SURNAME	CHR. NAME	AGE	BIRTH PLACE	CENSUS PARISH	BOOK	PG
DAVIDSON	Isabel	74	Forglen	Forglen	1	1
DAVIDSON	James	7mths	Alvah	Inverkeithny	2	4
DAVIDSON	James	74	Forgue ABD	Marnoch	8	4
DAVIDSON	Jane	2	Marnoch	Marnoch	9	7
DAVIDSON	Jane	56	Marnoch	Marnoch	7	3
DAVIDSON	Joseph	40	Marnoch	Marnoch	6	15
DAVIDSON	Margaret	10	Marnoch	Marnoch	6	28
DAVIDSON	Mary	10	Alvah	Marnoch	6	15
DAVIDSON	Mary	38	Ordiquhill	Marnoch	7	10
DAVIDSON	Mary	33	Auchterless ABD	Forglen	1	8
DAVIDSON	Mary	30	Marnoch	Marnoch	6	15
DAVIDSON	Mina	11mths	Marnoch	Marnoch	7	1
DAVIDSON	William	1	Marnoch	Marnoch	6	15
DAVIDSON	William	40	Monquhitter ABD	Marnoch	7	1
DAVIDSON?	female	2mths	Marnoch	Marnoch	9	7
DAWSON	Alexander	29	Strathdon ABD	Inverkeithny	2	5
DAWSON	Alexander W.	30	Banff	Marnoch	1	7
DAWSON	George	49	Marnoch	Marnoch	3	8
DAWSON	George	17	Marnoch	Marnoch	3	11
DAWSON	Helen	42	Inverkeithny	Inverkeithny	1	4
DAWSON	Isabella	3	Cairnie ABD	Marnoch	3	12
DAWSON	Isobel	7	Marnoch	Marnoch	3	8
DAWSON	James	5	Forglen	Forglen	2	3
DAWSON	Jane	47	Greenock RFW	Marnoch	3	8
DAWSON	Jane	12	Marnoch	Marnoch	7	8
DAWSON	Jean Ward	25	Auchterless ABD	Forglen	2	6
DAWSON	John	32	Alvah	Marnoch	2	2
DAWSON	Mary	3	Forglen	Forglen	2	3
DAWSON	Robert	27	Aberdeen ABD	Inverkeithny	2	5
DAWSON	William	9	Marnoch	Marnoch	3	8
DAY	Jean	15	Boyndie	Marnoch	5	5
DEAN	Alexander	70	Forgue ABD	Inverkeithny	2	11
DEAN	Alexander	9	Aberdeen ABD	Inverkeithny	2	11
DEAN	Charles	25	Inverkeithny	Inverkeithny	2	11
DEAN	Isabella	24	Inverkeithny	Inverkeithny	2	11
DEAN	James	13	Forglen	Forglen	4	3
DEAN	Jean	65	Inverkeithny	Inverkeithny	2	11
DEAN	Mary	5	Marnoch	Marnoch	9	5
DEMPSTER	Agnes	3	Alvah	Marnoch	6	24
DEMPSTER	Arthur	53	Inverkeithny	Inverkeithny	3	7
DEMPSTER	Elizabeth	5	Inverkeithny	Inverkeithny	3	7
DEMPSTER	George	9	Inverkeithny	Inverkeithny	3	7
DEMPSTER	Helen	26	Inverkeithny	Inverkeithny	3	7
DEMPSTER	James	13	Inverkeithny	Inverkeithny	3	2
DEMPSTER	Mary	50	King Edward ABD	Inverkeithny	3	7
DEMPSTER	Susan	25	Auchterless ABD	Forglen	4	1
DEY	George	37	Cairnie ABD	Marnoch	3	15
DICK	Ann	9	Marnoch	Marnoch	5	24
DICK	Christian	6	Marnoch	Marnoch	5	24
DICK	Harriet	17	Turriff ABD	Forglen	3	5
DICK	Jean	40	Marnoch	Marnoch	5	24
DICK	Jean	20	Marnoch	Marnoch	5	24
DICK	Mary	5mths	Marnoch	Marnoch	5	24
DICK	William	4	Marnoch	Marnoch	5	24
DICK	William	46	Culross PER	Marnoch	5	24
DICKIE	Mary	35	Inverkeithny	Marnoch	7	13
DICKIE	William	3	Boyndie	Marnoch	7	13
DINGWALL	Agnes	7	Turriff ABD	Forglen	1	2
DINGWALL	Alexander	1	Banff	Marnoch	7	7
DINGWALL	Alexander	4	Turriff ABD	Forglen	1	2
DINGWALL	Alexander	29	Marnoch	Marnoch	4	4
DINGWALL	Alexander	63	Marnoch	Marnoch	6	3
DINGWALL	Archibald	3mths	Forglen	Forglen	1	2
DINGWALL	George	2	Turriff ABD	Forglen	1	2

SURNAME	CHR. NAME	AGE	BIRTH PLACE	CENSUS PARISH	BOOK	PG
DINGWALL	George	40	Gamrie	Marnoch	7	7
DINGWALL	George	6	Banff	Marnoch	7	7
DINGWALL	Helen	3	Banff	Marnoch	7	7
DINGWALL	Isabella	39	Deskford	Marnoch	7	7
DINGWALL	James	40	Monquhitter ABD	Forglen	1	1
DINGWALL	Jane	8	Banff	Marnoch	7	7
DINGWALL	Jane	71	Marnoch	Marnoch	6	3
DINGWALL	Joseph	12	Auchterless ABD	Forglen	1	2
DINGWALL	Margaret	66	Forglen	Marnoch	4	4
DINGWALL	Margaret	31	Marnoch	Marnoch	4	4
DINGWALL	Margaret	12	Banff	Marnoch	7	7
DINGWALL	Margaret	39	Turriff ABD	Forglen	1	1
DINGWALL	Mary	9	Turriff ABD	Forglen	1	2
DINGWALL	William	10	Banff	Marnoch	7	7
DINGWALL	William	66	Marnoch	Marnoch	4	4
DONALD	Alexander	18	Rathven	Forglen	2	7
DONALD	James	19	Fordyce	Marnoch	5	6
DONALD	John	26	Boyndie	Marnoch	1	1
DONALD	John	28	Huntly ABD	Marnoch	4	5
DONALD	Margaret	98	Marnoch	Marnoch	7	1
DONALD	Mary	58	Forglen	Marnoch	5	26
DONALD	William	20	King Edward ABD	Inverkeithny	2	12
DONALD	William	17	Monquhitter ABD	Marnoch	8	5
DONALDSON	Ann	57	Cairnie ABD	Marnoch	6	21
DONALDSON	Anne	17	Forglen	Marnoch	3	12
DONALDSON	Catherine	19	Elgin MOR	Marnoch	8	1
DONALDSON	George	47	Forglen	Forglen	1	1
DONALDSON	George	5	Marnoch	Marnoch	5	23
DONALDSON	George	33	Logie Buchan ABD	Forglen	1	8
DONALDSON	Gordon	22	Forglen	Marnoch	4	9
DONALDSON	Helen	14	Forglen	Marnoch	6	21
DONALDSON	Jane	25	Forglen	Marnoch	7	6
DONALDSON	Janet	2	Marnoch	Marnoch	5	23
DONALDSON	Jean	10	Alvah	Marnoch	5	23
DONALDSON	Jean	14	Grange	Marnoch	1	2
DOUGLAS	Adam	6	Inverkeithny	Inverkeithny	1	3
DOUGLAS	Donald	38	Ferintosh ROC	Inverkeithny	1	3
DOUGLAS	Isabella	38	Jedburgh ROX	Inverkeithny	1	3
DOUGLAS	Isabella	13	Huntly ABD	Marnoch	2	7
DOUGLAS	John	23	Ferintosh ROC	Inverkeithny	1	3
DOUGLAS	William	46	Ferintosh ROC	Inverkeithny	1	3
DOW	Charles	44	Turriff ABD	Marnoch	8	2
DOW	Christian	14	Marnoch	Marnoch	9	1
DOW	Elizabeth	16	Forgue ABD	Inverkeithny	2	16
DOW	Elspet	50	Fordyce	Marnoch	9	1
DOW	Elspet	17	Marnoch	Inverkeithny	2	1
DOW	James	21	Marnoch	Marnoch	9	1
DOW	Jane	25	Marnoch	Marnoch	5	20
DOW	Jessie	46	Forglen	Marnoch	8	2
DOW	John	52	Forgue ABD	Marnoch	9	1
DOW	John R.	29	Inverkeithny	Inverkeithny	2	16
DOW	Joseph	8	Marnoch	Marnoch	9	1
DOW	Margaret	28	Alvah	Marnoch	5	4
DOW	Sally	20	Marnoch	Marnoch	9	1
DOWNEY	Betty	52	Marnoch	Marnoch	6	12
DOWNEY	Betty	23	Marnoch	Marnoch	6	12
DOWNEY	Jane	21	Marnoch	Marnoch	6	12
DRUMMOND	Catherine	6	Marnoch	Marnoch	9	9
DRUMMOND	Hannah	31	Marnoch	Marnoch	9	9
DRUMMOND	Hannah	4	Marnoch	Marnoch	9	9
DRUMMOND	James	30	Fort George INV	Marnoch	9	9
DRUMMOND	James	1	Marnoch	Marnoch	9	9
DUFF	Benjamin	11	Ireland	Marnoch	3	10
DUFF	Helen	8	Marnoch	Marnoch	3	10

SURNAME	CHR. NAME	AGE	BIRTH PLACE	CENSUS PARISH	BOOK	PG
DUFF	Helen	20	Ordiquhill	Marnoch	2	2
DUFF	John	8	Marnoch	Marnoch	3	10
DUFF	Mary	10	Marnoch	Marnoch	3	10
DUFF	Mary	21	Fordyce	Inverkeithny	1	6
DUFFUS	Alexander	33	Inverkeithny	Marnoch	5	6
DUFFUS	Catherine	26	Inverkeithny	Inverkeithny	3	14
DUFFUS	Elizabeth	21	Inverkeithny	Inverkeithny	3	14
DUFFUS	George	20	Forgue ABD	Marnoch	9	1
DUFFUS	George	32	Inverkeithny	Inverkeithny	2	11
DUFFUS	George	78	Aberdeen ABD	Inverkeithny	3	14
DUFFUS	Helen	63	Inverkeithny	Inverkeithny	3	14
DUFFUS	Helen	11	Inverkeithny	Inverkeithny	3	14
DUFFUS	Isobel	2	Marnoch	Marnoch	5	6
DUFFUS	Jean	38	Gartly ABD	Inverkeithny	2	13
DUFFUS	Jean	4	Marnoch	Marnoch	5	6
DUFFUS	John	30	Inverkeithny	Inverkeithny	2	13
DUFFUS	John	41	Inverkeithny	Inverkeithny	3	14
DUFFUS	John	18	Forgue ABD	Inverkeithny	3	9
DUFFUS	Mary	3	Alvah	Inverkeithny	2	11
DUFFUS	Mary	61	Drumblade ABD	Inverkeithny	2	11
DUFFUS	William	24	Huntly ABD	Marnoch	9	1
DUNCAN	Alexander	51	Grange	Marnoch	7	14
DUNCAN	Alexander	18	Turriff ABD	Forglen	2	9
DUNCAN	Alexander	1	Banff	Marnoch	2	13
DUNCAN	Alexander	8	Forglen	Forglen	3	9
DUNCAN	Alexander	17	Gamrie	Forglen	4	4
DUNCAN	Ann	41	Marnoch	Marnoch	6	6
DUNCAN	Ann	18	Fordyce	Inverkeithny	2	2
DUNCAN	Barbara	29	Auchterless ABD	Forglen	2	1
DUNCAN	Barbara	17	Turriff ABD	Forglen	4	9
DUNCAN	Betty	15	Marnoch	Forglen	1	4
DUNCAN	Christian	27	Monqihitter ABD	Forglen	1	7
DUNCAN	Elizabeth	51	Inverkeithny	Inverkeithny	3	12
DUNCAN	Elspet	30	Boyndie	Marnoch	2	13
DUNCAN	Francis	14	Turriff ABD	Marnoch	6	8
DUNCAN	George	35	King Edward ABD	Marnoch	2	12
DUNCAN	George	7	Boyndie	Marnoch	2	13
DUNCAN	George	55	Inverkeithny	Inverkeithny	3	12
DUNCAN	Isabel	25	Rothiemay	Forglen	1	9
DUNCAN	Isabel	39	Udny ABD	Forglen	4	4
DUNCAN	Isabel	10	Fintray ABD	Inverkeithny	2	14
DUNCAN	Isabel	52	Keithhall ABD	Inverkeithny	2	14
DUNCAN	Isabella	51	Grange	Forglen	3	9
DUNCAN	James	5	Banff	Marnoch	2	13
DUNCAN	James	50	Keithhall ABD	Inverkeithny	2	14
DUNCAN	Jane	12	Marnoch	Marnoch	6	6
DUNCAN	Jane Ann	10	Ellon ABD	Forglen	4	4
DUNCAN	Janet	18	Turriff ABD	Marnoch	1	14
DUNCAN	Jean	8	Auchterless ABD	Forglen	2	1
DUNCAN	John	20	Monquhitter ABD	Forglen	3	2
DUNCAN	John	4mths	Forglen	Forglen	4	4
DUNCAN	John	61	Inverkeithny	Inverkeithny	3	12
DUNCAN	Margaret	3	Fordyce	Marnoch	7	14
DUNCAN	Margaret	53	Cairnie ABD	Marnoch	7	14
DUNCAN	Robert	8	Ellon ABD	Forglen	4	4
DUNCAN	Robert	40	Old Deer ABD	Forglen	4	4
DUNCAN	William	10	Forglen	Forglen	3	9
DUNCAN	William	6mths	Keith	Marnoch	7	11
DUNCAN	William	10	Marnoch	Marnoch	5	3
DUNCAN	William	79	Marnoch	Marnoch	7	6
DUNDAS	Ann	5	Inverkeithny	Inverkeithny	3	15
DUNDAS	Ann	31	Mortlach	Inverkeithny	3	14
DUNDAS	Isabella	3	Inverkeithny	Inverkeithny	3	15
DUNDAS	James	36	Keith	Inverkeithny	3	14

SURNAME	CHR. NAME	AGE	BIRTH PLACE	CENSUS PARISH	BOOK	PG
DUNDAS	James	69	Bellie MOR	Inverkeithny	3	14
DUNDAS	James	7	Inverkeithny	Inverkeithny	3	15
DUNDAS	Jean	8	Inverkeithny	Inverkeithny	3	14
DUNDAS	Marjory	1	Inverkeithny	Inverkeithny	3	15
DUNDAS	William	10	Inverkeithny	Inverkeithny	3	14
DURNO	Alexander	38	Auchincrow BEW	Marnoch	6	8
DURNO	George	8	Auchincrow BEW	Marnoch	6	8
DURNO	James	7	Auchincrow BEW	Marnoch	6	8
DURNO	Jane	2	Marnoch	Marnoch	6	8
DURNO	Janet	34	Innerwick ELN	Marnoch	6	8
DURNO	Jessie	11	Auchincrow BEW	Marnoch	6	8
DURNO	Thomas	4	Marnoch	Marnoch	6	8
DUSTON	Mary	18	Forgue ABD	Inverkeithny	2	3
DYKER	Agnes	9	Inverkeithny	Inverkeithny	1	10
DYKER	Alexander	39	Inverkeithny	Marnoch	6	1
DYKER	Alexander	9	Marnoch	Marnoch	6	1
DYKER	Elspet	8	Inverkeithny	Inverkeithny	1	10
DYKER	George	12	Inverkeithny	Inverkeithny	1	7
DYKER	Helen	3	Marnoch	Marnoch	6	1
DYKER	Helen	32	Marnoch	Marnoch	6	1
DYKER	James	48	Cairnie ABD	Inverkeithny	1	10
DYKER	Margaret	46	Huntly ABD	Inverkeithny	1	10
DYKER	Peter	8	Inverkeithny	Inverkeithny	2	9
DYKER	Robert	5	Inverkeithny	Inverkeithny	1	10
DYKER	William	5	Marnoch	Marnoch	6	1
EARCHLAT	John	23	Huntly ABD	Forglen	2	8
EDWARDS	Alexander	30	Marnoch	Marnoch	7	4
EDWARDS	Isobel	67	Marnoch	Marnoch	7	4
EDWARDS	Jane	24	Marnoch	Marnoch	7	4
EDWARDS	Jean	25	Keith	Forglen	3	8
EDWARDS	John	73	Forgue ABD	Marnoch	7	4
ELDER	Helen	23	Inverkeithny	Inverkeithny	1	8
ELDER	Isabella	40	Grange	Marnoch	6	1
ELDER	Isabella	10	Inverkeithny	Inverkeithny	1	8
ELDER	James	21	Marnoch	Inverkeithny	3	2
ELDER	James	61	Marnoch	Inverkeithny	1	8
ELDER	Robert	13	Inverkeithny	Inverkeithny	1	8
ELDER	William	7-	Grange	Marnoch	6	1
ELDER	William	29	Inverkeithny	Inverkeithny	1	8
ELLICE	Alexander	24	Culsalmond ABD	Inverkeithny	2	15
ELLICE	Alexander	65	Forgue ABD	Inverkeithny	2	15
ELLICE	Edward	19	Culsalmond ABD	Inverkeithny	2	15
ELLICE	Elspet	55	Marnoch	Inverkeithny	2	15
ELLICE	Helen	30	Boyndie	Marnoch	7	11
ELLICE	Jean	12	Culsalmond ABD	Inverkeithny	2	16
ELLICE	Mary	20	Culsalmond ABD	Inverkeithny	2	15
ELLIS	Bartlet	5	Banff	Marnoch	7	11
ELLIS	Betty	9	Banff	Marnoch	7	11
ELLIS	Duff	33	Banff	Marnoch	7	11
ELLIS	James	9	Banff	Marnoch	7	11
ELLIS	Margaret	3	Banff	Marnoch	7	11
ELLIS	Sophia	7	Banff	Marnoch	7	11
ELMSLIE	Elizabeth	34	Turriff ABD	Forglen	1	4
ELMSLIE	Elsie	12	Banff	Forglen	1	4
ELRICK	James	18	New Deer ABD	Inverkeithny	2	7
ENGLAND	Ann	29	Marnoch	Marnoch	9	10
ENGLAND	Ann	5	Marnoch	Marnoch	5	1
ENGLAND	Christian	7	Marnoch	Marnoch	5	1
ENGLAND	George	9	Marnoch	Marnoch	9	10
ENGLAND	Mary	3	Forglen	Inverkeithny	2	9
ENGLAND	William	7	Marnoch	Marnoch	9	10
EWAN	Alexander	5	Marnoch	Marnoch	6	19
EWAN	Alexander	55	Marnoch	Marnoch	6	20
EWAN	Elizabeth	5	Alvah	Marnoch	6	20

SURNAME	CHR. NAME	AGE	BIRTH PLACE	CENSUS PARISH	BOOK	PG
EWAN	Elizabeth	57	Marnoch	Marnoch	6	20
EWAN	Elspet	1	Marnoch	Marnoch	6	19
EWAN	Margaret	27	Ordiquhill	Marnoch	6	19
EWAN	William	30	Marnoch	Marnoch	6	19
EWEN	Ann	7	Fordyce	Marnoch	2	8
EWEN	James	30	Marnoch	Inverkeithny	1	10
EWEN	John	18	Marnoch	Inverkeithny	1	10
EWING	John	10	Marnoch	Marnoch	6	1
EWING	Margaret	68	Fordyce	Marnoch	6	10
Earchlat	Jn	23	Huntly ABD	Forglen	2	8
Edwards	Jean	25	Keith	Forglen	3	8
Elmslie	Eliz.	34	Turriff ABD	Forglen	1	4
Elmslie	Elsie	12	Banff	Forglen	1	4
FALLEN	Alexander	6	Alvah	Marnoch	6	24
FARSKIN	Isobel	43	Inverkeithny	Marnoch	6	28
FARSKIN	Jean	11	Forgue ABD	Marnoch	5	7
FARSKIN	Margaret	50	Inverkeithny	Marnoch	6	28
FEICH	Jean	16	Marnoch	Marnoch	4	16
FERGUSON	George	27	Stirling STI	Inverkeithny	1	2
FIDDES	Alexander	13	Old Machar ABD	Marnoch	1	10
FIDDES	William	16	Old Machar ABD	Marnoch	1	10
FIDDLER	Eliza	6	Marnoch	Marnoch	6	24
FIDDLER	John	17	Marnoch	Marnoch	6	23
FIDDLER	Mary	8	Marnoch	Marnoch	6	23
FINDLATER	Helen	60	Forglen	Marnoch	5	23
FINDLATER	James	21	Marnoch	Marnoch	5	12
FINDLATER	Jessie	57	New Deer ABD	Marnoch	6	6
FINDLATER	Margaret	30	Marnoch	Marnoch	5	23
FINDLATER	Margaret	19	Marnoch	Marnoch	5	12
FINDLATER	Margaret	53	Turriff ABD	Marnoch	5	12
FINDLATER	Mary	12	Marnoch	Marnoch	5	12
FINDLATER	Peter	25	Aberdeen ABD	Marnoch	5	12
FINDLATER	Peter	5	Forglen	Marnoch	9	11
FINDLATER	Peter	74	-	Marnoch	5	12
FINDLATER?	Charles	17	Marnoch	Marnoch	9	8
FINDLAY	Jane S.	22	Marnoch	Marnoch	6	17
FINDLAY	Janet	51	New Deer ABD	Marnoch	6	17
FINNIE	Alexander	2	Inverkeithny	Inverkeithny	3	3
FINNIE	Alexander	69	Gamrie	Marnoch	4	5
FINNIE	Ann	4	Inverkeithny	Inverkeithny	3	3
FINNIE	Francis	35	New Deer ABD	Inverkeithny	3	2
FINNIE	Francis	9	Inverkeithny	Inverkeithny	3	2
FINNIE	James	11	Inverkeithny	Inverkeithny	3	2
FINNIE	Jane	34	Mortlach	Inverkeithny	3	2
FINNIE	Jean	34	Auchterless ABD	Marnoch	4	5
FINNIE	John	7	Inverkeithny	Inverkeithny	3	2
FINNIE	Margaret	36	Auchterless ABD	Marnoch	4	5
FINNIE	Mary	9	Turriff ABD	Marnoch	4	5
FINNIE	Peter	10mths	Inverkeithny	Inverkeithny	3	3
FINNY	Ann	40	Auchterless ABD	Marnoch	5	25
FLAMING	Peter	65	Inveravon	Marnoch	2	5
FLEMING	Charles	30	Glenmuick ABD	Inverkeithny	1	10
FLEMING	Janet	57	Inveravon	Marnoch	2	5
FLETCHER	Isabella	24	Banff	Marnoch	4	8
FLORENCE	Ann	9mths	King Edward ABD	Inverkeithny	3	8
FORBES	Adam	21	Huntly ABD	Inverkeithny	2	3
FORBES	Barbara	14	Rothiemay	Marnoch	2	9
FORBES	Catherine	62	Insch ABD	Marnoch	6	19
FORBES	Finlay	28	Blair Athol PER	Marnoch	6	11
FORBES	George	26	Forgue ABD	Inverkeithny	2	9
FORBES	John	11	Cairnie ABD	Marnoch	7	13
FORBES	John	2	Marnoch	Marnoch	6	1
FORBES	Margaret	29	Banff	Marnoch	6	4
FORBES	Mary	5	Marnoch	Marnoch	6	4

SURNAME	CHR. NAME	AGE	BIRTH PLACE	CENSUS PARISH	BOOK	PG
FORBES	Mary	8mths	Inverkeithny	Inverkeithny	3	14
FORBES	Susan	2	Marnoch	Marnoch	6	4
FORBES	William	32	Rothiemay	Marnoch	2	12
FORDYCE	Alexander	20	Marnoch	Inverkeithny	3	10
FORDYCE	Charles	2	Marnoch	Marnoch	2	12
FORDYCE	Isabella	46	Marnoch	Marnoch	2	12
FORDYCE	Isabella	16	Marnoch	Marnoch	2	12
FORDYCE	James	49	Marnoch	Marnoch	2	13
FORDYCE	James	12	Marnoch	Marnoch	2	12
FORDYCE	John	5	Marnoch	Marnoch	2	12
FORDYCE	John	44	Rothiemay	Marnoch	2	12
FORDYCE	Margaret	10mths	Marnoch	Marnoch	1	12
FORDYCE	Margaret	29	Forgue ABD	Marnoch	1	12
FORDYCE	Margaret	8	Marnoch	Marnoch	2	10
FORDYCE	William	10	Marnoch	Marnoch	2	12
FORDYCE	William	49	Marnoch	Marnoch	1	12
FORDYCE	William	61	Marnoch	Marnoch	4	15
FOREST	Isabella	17	Deskford	Marnoch	1	14
FORSYTH	Donald	23	Ferintosh ROC	Inverkeithny	1	3
FORSYTH	John	17	Boyndie	Marnoch	4	16
FOWLER	Elspet	12	Fyvie ABD	Marnoch	8	3
FOWLER	William	26	Ferintosh ROC	Inverkeithny	1	3
FOWLIE	Isabella	10mths	Inverkeithny	Inverkeithny	3	3
FOWLIE	Isabella	36	Auchterless ABD	Inverkeithny	3	3
FOWLIE	John	50	Turriff ABD	Inverkeithny	3	3
FRASER	Alexander	33	Abernethy BAN	Marnoch	2	3
FRASER	Alexander	21	Ordiquhill	Marnoch	9	8
FRASER	George	10mths	Marnoch	Marnoch	3	9
FRASER	Isabella	17	Boyndie	Marnoch	3	12
FRASER	Jean	35	Cullen	Marnoch	1	2
FRASER	John	9	Drumblade ABD	Marnoch	3	9
FRASER	John	30	Inverness INV	Marnoch	5	21
FRASER	Margaret	7	Banff	Marnoch	3	9
FRASER	Margaret	57	Urquhart MOR	Marnoch	7	13
FRASER	Mary	34	Fordyce	Marnoch	3	9
FRASER	Robert	27	Ordiquhill	Marnoch	8	11
FRASER	Simon	21	Turriff ABD	Marnoch	3	2
FRASER	Thomas	31	Ordiquhill	Marnoch	1	2
FRASER	William	15	Alvah	Inverkeithny	2	8
FRASER	William	5	Marnoch	Marnoch	3	9
FRASER	William	37	Forglen	Marnoch	3	9
FRAZER	John	35	Ordiquhill	Marnoch	6	20
FYFE	Charles	23	Turriff ABD	Inverkeithny	2	14
Fairweather	Ann	29	Forglen	Forglen	4	8
Fairweather	James	34	Forglen	Forglen	4	8
Fairweather	Jean	32	Forglen	Forglen	4	8
Ferguson	Margt	21	Monquhitter Abd.	Forglen	1	6
Fife	Margt	22	Gamrie	Forglen	4	7
Findlater	Alex	9	Forglen	Forglen	2	11
Findlater	Alex	27	Forglen	Forglen	2	11
Findlater	Alex	35	Forglen	Forglen	2	4
Findlater	Ann	21	Auchterless ABD	Forglen	2	11
Findlater	Ann	1	Forglen	Forglen	2	11
Findlater	Ann	84	Aberdour ABD	Forglen	2	3
Findlater	Helen	68	Marnoch	Forglen	2	4
Findlater	Helen	45	King Edward ABD	Forglen	2	3
Findlater	Isabella	2mths	Forglen	Forglen	2	11
Findlater	Isabella	18	Marnoch	Forglen	3	4
Findlater	Isabella	58	Rothiemay	Forglen	3	8
Findlater	James	10	Turriff ABD	Forglen	2	4
Findlater	James	29	Forglen	Forglen	3	8
Findlater	Jean	8	Marnoch	Forglen	2	11
Findlater	Jean	3	Forglen	Forglen	2	11
Findlater	Margt	5	Forglen	Forglen	2	11

SURNAME	CHR. NAME	AGE	BIRTH PLACE	CENSUS PARISH	BOOK	PG
Findlater	Mary	22	Monquhitter ABD	Forglen	2	11
Findlater	Patrick	10	Forglen	Forglen	3	8
Findlater	Robert	4	Monquhitter ABD	Forglen	3	8
Findlater	Wm	33	Forglen	Forglen	2	11
Findlater	Wm	63	King Edward ABD	Forglen	3	8
Forbes	Margt	22	Cairnie	Forglen	2	9
Forsyth	Jane	23	Auchterless ABD	Forglen	1	8
Foset	Peter	39	Meek? Galloway	Forglen	3	2
Fraser	Eliz.	11	Monquhitter ABD	Forglen	2	8
Fraser	Eliz.	17	Durris KCD	Forglen	3	7
Fraser	Isabella	12	Ordiquhill	Forglen	3	1
Fraser	James	72	Westruther BEW	Forglen	1	7
Fraser	Jean	10	Durris KCD	Forglen	3	7
Fraser	Jean	41	Gardenstown	Forglen	2	8
Fraser	Jean	50	Kinellan ABD	Forglen	3	7
Fraser	Jn	18	Monquhitter ABD	Forglen	2	10
Fraser	Margt	21	Turriff	Forglen	1	7
Fraser	Margt	7	Durris KCD	Forglen	3	7
Fraser	Thomas	15	Durris KCD	Forglen	3	7
Fraser	Wm	45	Gardenstown	Forglen	2	8
Fraser	Wm	50	Kincardine O'Neil ABD	Forglen	3	7
Frigg	Ann	6	Forglen	Forglen	2	1
Frigg	Charles	1	Forglen	Forglen	2	1
Frigg	Elspet	38	Elgin MOR	Forglen	2	1
Frigg	Robert	4	Forglen	Forglen	2	1
Frigg	Wm	38	Urquhart MOR	Forglen	2	1
Frigg	Wm	8	Urquhart MOR	Forglen	2	1
GAIR	Donald	39	Logie ROC	Marnoch	5	9
GAIR	Isabella	36	Urquhart ROC	Marnoch	5	9
GAIR	John	10	Marnoch	Marnoch	5	9
GALL	Alexander	17	Ordiquhill	Marnoch	1	1
GALL	Alexander	23	Marnoch	Marnoch	7	5
GAMMACK	Alexander	13	Marnoch	Marnoch	5	4
GAMMACK	Ann	42	Marnoch	Marnoch	5	3
GAMMACK	Harvey	1	Marnoch	Marnoch	5	4
GAMMACK	Jacobina	58	Forgue ABD	Marnoch	6	2
GAMMACK	James	9	Marnoch	Marnoch	5	4
GAMMACK	James	54	Turriff	Marnoch	5	3
GAMMACK	John E.	4	Marnoch	Marnoch	5	4
GAMMACK	Ramsey	1	Marnoch	Marnoch	5	4
GAMMACK	William	7	Marnoch	Marnoch	5	4
GAMMIE	Agnes	92	Marnoch	Marnoch	2	10
GAMMIE	Agnes	12	Marnoch	Marnoch	2	10
GAMMIE	Agnes	48	Marnoch	Marnoch	2	10
GAMMIE	Ann	61	Inverkeithny	Marnoch	4	3
GAMMIE	Barbara	28	Marnoch	Marnoch	4	3
GAMMIE	Elspet	69	Marnoch	Marnoch	5	19
GAMMIE	Elspet	15	Forgue ABD	Inverkeithny	2	11
GAMMIE	Helen	21	Marnoch	Marnoch	5	9
GAMMIE	James	56	Marnoch	Marnoch	5	9
GAMMIE	Jane	49	Marnoch	Marnoch	2	13
GAMMIE	Jane	20	Boyndie	Marnoch	2	9
GAMMIE	John	50	Marnoch	Marnoch	3	6
GAMMIE	Margaret	28	Boyndie	Marnoch	2	9
GAMMIE	Margaret	55	Boyndie	Marnoch	2	9
GAMMIE	Peter	9	Marnoch	Marnoch	3	6
GAMMIE	William	30	Marnoch	Marnoch	4	3
GAMMIE	William	55	Marnoch	Marnoch	2	9
GARDEN	Adam	23	Auchterless ABD	Inverkeithny	2	15
GARDEN	Jessie	33	Auchterless ABD	Inverkeithny	2	15
GARDINER	Isobel	17	Deskford	Marnoch	1	4
GARIOCH	Helen	7	Marnoch	Marnoch	3	1
GARLAND	Agnes	30	Alvah	Marnoch	6	24
GAUL	Alexander	19	Marnoch	Marnoch	4	10

SURNAME	CHR. NAME	AGE	BIRTH PLACE	CENSUS PARISH	BOOK	PG
GAUL	Margaret	45	Forgue ABD	Marnoch	6	16
GAULD	Alexander	53	Gartly ABD	Marnoch	5	23
GAULD	Alexander	1	Marnoch	Marnoch	5	23
GAULD	Alexander	6	Inverkeithny	Inverkeithny	1	9
GAULD	Alexander	63	Rothiemay	Inverkeithny	1	9
GAULD	Barbara	11	Inverkeithny	Inverkeithny	2	8
GAULD	Elspet	11	Inverkeithny	Inverkeithny	1	9
GAULD	Helen	3	Marnoch	Marnoch	5	23
GAULD	Janet	32	Gartly ABD	Marnoch	5	23
GAULD	Jean	9	Inverkeithny	Inverkeithny	1	9
GAULD	Jean	8	Inverkeithny	Inverkeithny	2	8
GAULD	Margaret	49	Cromdale MOR	Inverkeithny	1	9
GAULD	Martha	46	Fyvie ABD	Inverkeithny	2	8
GAULD	Peter	44	Rothiemay	Inverkeithny	2	8
GAULD	Sarah	13	Inverkeithny	Inverkeithny	2	8
GAULD	William	17	Inverkeithny	Inverkeithny	3	4
GEDDES	Elspet	10mths	Marnoch	Marnoch	6	13
GEDDES	George	5	Forglen	Marnoch	6	13
GEDDES	George	32	Marnoch	Marnoch	6	13
GEDDES	Helen	40	Forgue ABD	Marnoch	6	13
GEDDES	Janet	67	Fordyce	Marnoch	6	4
GEDDES	William	67	Rathven	Marnoch	6	4
GEEKIE	Elizabeth	18	Forgue ABD	Marnoch	9	6
GEORGE	Ann	85	Marnoch	Marnoch	6	20
GEORGE	Ann	23	Fyvie ABD	Inverkeithny	2	13
GEORGE	Janet	67	Drumblade ABD	Marnoch	5	2
GEORGE	Sarah	50	Bath ENG	Marnoch	5	24
GERARD	Christian	8	King Edward ABD	Inverkeithny	2	7
GERARD	Cobden(female)	4	King Edward ABD	Inverkeithny	2	7
GERRARD	Isobel	55	Marnoch	Marnoch	3	10
GERRIE	Ann	50	Marnoch	Marnoch	1	3
GERRIE	Anne	20	Forglen	Marnoch	9	2
GERRIE	George	61	Forglen	Marnoch	1	3
GERRIE	Margaret	24	Forglen	Marnoch	1	3
GERRIE	Sarah	4	Marnoch	Marnoch	6	13
GERRIE	William	28	Forglen	Marnoch	1	3
GIBB	Isabella	9wks	Marnoch	Marnoch	5	7
GIBB	John	33	Keith	Marnoch	3	8
GIBB	John	28	Forgue ABD	Marnoch	5	7
GIBSON	Forbes	32	Towie ABD	Inverkeithny	2	2
GIGGIE	William	15	Forgue ABD	Marnoch	4	3
GILES	Jean	14	Forgue ABD	Inverkeithny	1	4
GILLESPIE	Jessie	11	Auchterless ABD	Inverkeithny	2	15
GILLS	George	5	Marnoch	Marnoch	6	11
GILLS	John	68	Marnoch	Marnoch	6	11
GLENNIE	Catherine	31	Marnoch	Inverkeithny	1	8
GLENNIE	Catherine	4	Inverkeithny	Inverkeithny	1	8
GLENNIE	George	1	Inverkeithny	Inverkeithny	1	8
GLENNIE	Jane	7	Inverkeithny	Inverkeithny	1	8
GLENNIE	Margaret	6	Inverkeithny	Inverkeithny	1	8
GLENNIE	William	36	Insch ABD	Inverkeithny	1	8
GORDON	Adam	25	Cabrach	Inverkeithny	2	12
GORDON	Agnes	12	Marnoch	Marnoch	1	9
GORDON	Alexander	35	Gartly ABD	Marnoch	2	14
GORDON	Alexander	52	Grange	Marnoch	6	9
GORDON	Andrew	22	Aberdour ABD	Inverkeithny	2	5
GORDON	Ann	6mths	Inverkeithny	Inverkeithny	2	13
GORDON	Ann	9mths	Marnoch	Marnoch	8	1
GORDON	Ann	11	Marnoch	Marnoch	5	13
GORDON	Cahrles	30	King Edward ABD	Marnoch	6	2
GORDON	Catherine	4	Marnoch	Marnoch	6	28
GORDON	Charles	9	Marnoch	Marnoch	6	2
GORDON	Charles	16	Marnoch	Marnoch	5	13
GORDON	Elizabeth	36	Aberdeen ABD	Marnoch	6	2

SURNAME	CHR. NAME	AGE	BIRTH PLACE	CENSUS PARISH	BOOK	PG
GORDON	Elizabeth	3	Marnoch	Marnoch	6	2
GORDON	George	9	East Indies	Marnoch	8	1
GORDON	George	59	Tyrie ABD	Inverkeithny	2	5
GORDON	George	21	Marnoch	Marnoch	5	13
GORDON	Helen	7	Marnoch	Marnoch	6	28
GORDON	Isabella	30	Kennethmont? ABD	Marnoch	8	6
GORDON	Isabella	5	Marnoch	Marnoch	6	2
GORDON	Isobel	4	Marnoch	Marnoch	6	9
GORDON	James	5mths	Marnoch	Marnoch	2	14
GORDON	James	23	Marnoch	Marnoch	5	13
GORDON	James	14	Marnoch	Marnoch	5	20
GORDON	James	20	Aberdour ABD	Inverkeithny	2	5
GORDON	Jane	60	Keith	Marnoch	9	1
GORDON	Jane	18	Marnoch	Marnoch	5	13
GORDON	Jane	7	Marnoch	Marnoch	6	2
GORDON	Jane	11	Marnoch	Marnoch	6	9
GORDON	Jane	48	Monquhitter ABD	Inverkeithny	3	1
GORDON	Jane	25	Auchindoir ABD	Marnoch	2	14
GORDON	Jean	53	Marnoch	Marnoch	5	20
GORDON	Jessie	5	Auchindoir ABD	Marnoch	2	14
GORDON	John	9	Marnoch	Marnoch	9	5
GORDON	John	79	Forgue ABD	Marnoch	1	13
GORDON	Margaret	44	St Andrews-Llanbryde MOR	Marnoch	8	1
GORDON	Margaret	3	Auchindoir ABD	Marnoch	2	14
GORDON	Mary	41	Rhynie ABD	Marnoch	6	9
GORDON	Mary	6	Marnoch	Marnoch	5	13
GORDON	Mary M.	12	East Indies	Marnoch	8	1
GORDON	Peter	16	Aberchirder	Inverkeithny	3	12
GORDON	Susan	21	Forgue ABD	Inverkeithny	2	13
GORDON	William	46	Urquhart MOR	Marnoch	8	1
GORDON	William	10mths	Marnoch	Marnoch	6	2
GORDON	William	50	Drumblade ABD	Marnoch	5	12
GRAMT	William	46	Aberdeen ABD	Marnoch	3	13
GRANT	Alexander	18	Keith	Marnoch	2	12
GRANT	Alexander	40	Rothes MOR	Marnoch	1	7
GRANT	Alexander	12	Marnoch	Marnoch	5	16
GRANT	Alexander	12	Marnoch	Marnoch	3	13
GRANT	Andrew	14	Marnoch	Marnoch	1	7
GRANT	Ann	27	Forglen	Marnoch	6	21
GRANT	Ann	11	Marnoch	Marnoch	4	8
GRANT	Anne	37	Rothiemay	Marnoch	6	14
GRANT	Charles	8	Marnoch	Marnoch	3	13
GRANT	Christian	13	Marnoch	Marnoch	4	8
GRANT	Donald	6	Marnoch	Marnoch	1	7
GRANT	Donald	26	Inveravon	Marnoch	2	3
GRANT	Elizabeth	13	Huntly ABD	Marnoch	1	5
GRANT	Elspet	2	Marnoch	Marnoch	4	9
GRANT	George	26	Marnoch	Marnoch	7	7
GRANT	George	4	Marnoch	Marnoch	7	7
GRANT	George	36	Marnoch	Marnoch	4	8
GRANT	George	50	Huntly ABD	Marnoch	1	5
GRANT	Hay	30	Forglen	Inverkeithny	2	12
GRANT	Helen	38	Ordiquhill	Marnoch	1	7
GRANT	Helen	7	Marnoch	Marnoch	5	19
GRANT	Helen	14	Marnoch	Marnoch	3	13
GRANT	Isabella	62	Marnoch	Marnoch	7	7
GRANT	Isabella	17	Marnoch	Marnoch	3	13
GRANT	Isabella	2	Marnoch	Marnoch	4	8
GRANT	Isabella	26	Cairnie ABD	Marnoch	7	7
GRANT	Isabella	81	Rothiemay	Marnoch	6	14
GRANT	Isabella	38	Marnoch	Marnoch	4	8
GRANT	Isobel	5mths	Marnoch	Marnoch	3	3
GRANT	Isobel	16	Marnoch	Marnoch	3	2
GRANT	Isobel	6	Marnoch	Marnoch	1	5

SURNAME	CHR. NAME	AGE	BIRTH PLACE	CENSUS PARISH	BOOK	PG
GRANT	James	6	Marnoch	Marnoch	3	13
GRANT	James	54	Huntly ABD	Marnoch	5	16
GRANT	Jane	1	Marnoch	Marnoch	5	21
GRANT	Jane	8	Huntly ABD	Marnoch	1	5
GRANT	Jane	38	Marnoch	Marnoch	9	1
GRANT	Jane	9	Marnoch	Marnoch	9	1
GRANT	Janet	10	Huntly ABD	Marnoch	1	5
GRANT	Janet	47	Botriphnie	Marnoch	1	5
GRANT	Jean	15	Aberdeen ABD	Inverkeithny	3	15
GRANT	Jessie	10	Marnoch	Marnoch	4	11
GRANT	Jessie	17	Inverkeithny	Marnoch	4	3
GRANT	John	18	Inveravon	Marnoch	2	3
GRANT	John	15	Huntly ABD	Marnoch	2	2
GRANT	John	24	Inveravon	Marnoch	2	3
GRANT	Ludovick W.	10	Marnoch	Marnoch	1	7
GRANT	Margaret	5	Old Machar ABD	Marnoch	5	18
GRANT	Mary	18	Marnoch	Marnoch	7	7
GRANT	Mary	59	Devonshire	Marnoch	2	2
GRANT	Mary	50	Marnoch	Marnoch	6	6
GRANT	Robert	11mths	Marnoch	Marnoch	7	8
GRANT	William	82	Kirkmichael	Marnoch	6	21
GRANT	William	23	Marnoch	Marnoch	3	2
GRANT	William	7	Marnoch	Marnoch	4	8
GRANT	William	2	Marnoch	Marnoch	7	7
GRANT	William	11	Marnoch	Marnoch	7	5
GRANT	William	56	Forglen	Marnoch	7	7
GRANT	William	60	Inveravon	Marnoch	2	2
GRANT	george	4	Marnoch	Marnoch	4	8
GRANT	isabella	19	Alvah	Marnoch	4	3
GRANT?	female	3mths	Marnoch	Marnoch	6	21
GRAY	Alexander	24	Forgue ABD	Inverkeithny	1	4
GRAY	Alexander	22	Forglen	Marnoch	1	7
GRAY	Alexander	17	Deskford	Marnoch	1	14
GRAY	Anne	50	Turriff ABD	Marnoch	6	8
GRAY	Barbara	26	Marnoch	Marnoch	9	5
GRAY	Barbara	79	Forgue ABD	Marnoch	5	8
GRAY	Catherine	36	Marnoch	Marnoch	6	26
GRAY	Elizabeth	46	Lonmay ABD	Marnoch	5	2
GRAY	Elspet	32	Marnoch	Marnoch	2	2
GRAY	Elspet	62	Deskford	Marnoch	1	7
GRAY	George	15	Forgue ABD	Inverkeithny	3	14
GRAY	Isabel	68	Forgue ABD	Marnoch	5	25
GRAY	Isabella	7	Forgue ABD	Inverkeithny	2	15
GRAY	Isobel	37	Marnoch	Marnoch	9	5
GRAY	Isobel	33	Marnoch	Marnoch	5	2
GRAY	James	13	Banff	Inverkeithny	3	5
GRAY	James	36	Rothiemay	Inverkeithny	2	9
GRAY	James	56	Rothiemay	Marnoch	9	6
GRAY	James	17	Marnoch	Inverkeithny	3	10
GRAY	James	52	Turriff ABD	Marnoch	6	8
GRAY	James	51	Marnoch	Marnoch	4	11
GRAY	Jane	94	Alvah	Marnoch	6	4
GRAY	Jean	33	Marnoch	Inverkeithny	2	9
GRAY	John	23	Inverkeithny	Marnoch	8	10
GRAY	John	13	Forgue ABD	Inverkeithny	3	9
GRAY	John	29	Rothiemay	Marnoch	9	5
GRAY	John M.	3	Marnoch	Marnoch	9	6
GRAY	Margaret	53	Monquhitter ABD	Marnoch	6	8
GRAY	Margaret	39	Rhynie ABD	Marnoch	9	5
GRAY	Mary	10mths	Marnoch	Marnoch	9	6
GRAY	Robert	74	Forglen	Marnoch	9	5
GRAY	Roderick	30	Urquhart MOR	Inverkeithny	1	2
GRAY	William	26	Rothiemay	Inverkeithny	3	6
GRAY	William	16	Inverkeithny	Marnoch	9	1

SURNAME	CHR. NAME	AGE	BIRTH PLACE	CENSUS PARISH	BOOK	PG
GREENLAW	Janet	70	Marnoch	Marnoch	5	13
GREENLAW	Janet	66	Marnoch	Marnoch	6	14
GREENLAW	Maria	28	Marnoch	Marnoch	5	1
GREENLAW	Robert	56	Marnoch	Marnoch	5	1
GRIEVE	Ann	15	Inverkeithny	Inverkeithny	2	2
GUTHRIE	Agnes	9	Inverkeithny	Inverkeithny	3	11
GUTHRIE	Helen	49	Inverkeithny	Inverkeithny	3	11
GUTHRIE	Helen	13	Inverkeithny	Inverkeithny	3	11
GUTHRIE	James	22	Inverkeithny	Inverkeithny	3	11
GUTHRIE	James	50	Rothiemay	Inverkeithny	3	11
GUTHRIE	John	17	Inverkeithny	Inverkeithny	3	11
GUTHRIE	Peter	20	Inverkeithny	Inverkeithny	3	11
GUTHRIE	William	35	Culsalmond ABD	Marnoch	3	17
Gaul	Geo	19	Boyndie	Forglen	3	4
Gaul	Joseph	20	Boyndie	Forglen	3	4
Geddes	Alex	25	Fordyce	Forglen	2	9
Gerrard	Jn	17	Gamrie	Forglen	2	7
Gilgour	Agnes	7	Edinkillie MOR	Forglen	1	4
Gilgour	Jessie	3	Forglen	Forglen	1	4
Gilgour	Jessie Eliz.	37	Forglen	Forglen	1	4
Gilgour	Margt	60	Urquhart MOR	Forglen	1	4
Gilgour	Margt	5	Forglen	Forglen	1	4
Gilgour	Robert	35	Elgin MOR	Forglen	1	4
Gilgour	Robina Ann	11mths	Forglen	Forglen	1	4
Gill	Jean	23	King Edward ABD	Forglen	3	6
Gordon	Alex	50	England	Forglen	1	8
Gordon	Georgina I.	7	Auchterless ABD	Forglen	1	8
Gordon	Helen	2	Forglen	Forglen	4	1
Gordon	Jane	46	Aberdeen ABD	Forglen	1	8
Gordon	Jean	24	Cluny ABD	Forglen	3	7
Gordon	Wm	10	Forglen	Forglen	4	9
Gordon	Wm	85	Insch ABD	Forglen	3	7
Grant	Alex	40	Rothiemay	Forglen	3	5
Grant	Alex	10	Marnoch	Forglen	3	5
Grant	Geo	80	Grange	Forglen	1	5
Grant	Helen	34	Marnoch	Forglen	3	5
Grant	Isabel	86	Marnoch	Forglen	4	8
Grant	Isabella	33	Boharm	Forglen	2	9
Grant	James	12	Marnoch	Forglen	3	5
Grant	Jean	76	Forglen	Forglen	3	8
Grant	Margt	74	Grange	Forglen	1	5
Grant	Peter	36	Newrie AYR	Forglen	3	2
Gray	Alex	30	Boyndie	Forglen	2	3
Gray	Ann	21	Turriff ABD	Forglen	2	3
Gray	Ann	15	Montrose ANS	Forglen	3	3
Gray	Eliz	10	Forglen	Forglen	2	6
Gray	Elspet	73	Forglen	Forglen	2	2
Gray	Geo	1	Forglen	Forglen	2	3
Gray	James	41	Forglen	Forglen	2	6
Gray	Jane	71	Marnoch	Forglen	4	8
Gray	Wm	8	Forglen	Forglen	2	6
Greenlaw	Alex	66	Alvah	Forglen	3	2
Greenlaw	James	22	Alvah	Forglen	3	2
Greenlaw	Jn	4	Monquhitter ABD	Forglen	2	4
Greig	Alex	66	Dyce ABD	Forglen	4	4
Greig	Ann	33	Oyne ABD	Forglen	3	7
Greig	Christina	5	Turriff ABD	Forglen	3	7
Greig	Francis	32	Turriff ABD	Forglen	3	7
Greig	Geo	7	Turriff ABD	Forglen	3	7
Greig	Margt	55	New Machar ABD	Forglen	4	4
Greig	Mary	8	Turriff ABD	Forglen	3	7
Gudfellow	Margt	60	Montrose FORFAR	Forglen	3	9
HADDEN	Jessie	17	Marnoch	Marnoch	9	9
HADDIN	John	37	Lime Kilns FIF	Marnoch	6	23

SURNAME	CHR. NAME	AGE	BIRTH PLACE	CENSUS PARISH	BOOK	PG
HAGG	Elizabeth	36	Fetteresso KCD	Forglen	3	8
HALKET	John	21	Turriff ABD	Forglen	3	4
HALL	Alexander	9	Inverkeithny	Inverkeithny	2	16
HALL	Ann	14	Inverkeithny	Inverkeithny	3	2
HALL	Ann	78	Rothiemay	Marnoch	6	22
HALL	Barbara	11	Inverkeithny	Inverkeithny	2	16
HALL	Isabel	13	Turriff ABD	Forglen	2	2
HALL	Isabel	48	Old Machar ABD	Forglen	2	2
HALL	Isabella	22	Forgue ABD	Inverkeithny	2	16
HALL	Jane	20	Forgue ABD	Inverkeithny	2	16
HALL	Jean	8	Turriff ABD	Forglen	2	2
HALL	Margaret	17	Forgue ABD	Inverkeithny	2	16
HALL	Margaret	52	Forgue ABD	Inverkeithny	2	16
HALL	Margaret	10	Turriff ABD	Forglen	1	9
HALL	Mary	3	Turriff ABD	Forglen	2	2
HALL	Patrick	46	Forgue ABD	Inverkeithny	2	16
HALL	Walter	82	Insch ABD	Marnoch	6	22
HAMILTON	Isabel	9mths	Marnoch	Marnoch	1	3
HAMILTON	William	25	Marnoch	Forglen	4	9
HARPER	.Jean	3	Inverkeithny	Inverkeithny	1	6
HARPER	Alexander	3	Gamrie	Marnoch	1	8
HARPER	Alexander	34	Marnoch	Marnoch	9	10
HARPER	Alexander	48	Daviot ABD	Marnoch	1	8
HARPER	Alexander	71	Forgue ABD	Inverkeithny	2	9
HARPER	Alexander	23	Inverkeithny	Inverkeithny	2	9
HARPER	Ann	31	Inverkeithny	Inverkeithny	1	6
HARPER	Ann	79	Marnoch	Marnoch	3	3
HARPER	Ann	22	Auchterless ABD	Inverkeithny	2	9
HARPER	Anne	43	Culsalmond ABD	Marnoch	3	14
HARPER	Elizabeth	3	Forgue ABD	Inverkeithny	3	2
HARPER	Elizabeth	14	Marnoch	Marnoch	7	5
HARPER	Elspet	81	Marnoch	Marnoch	5	10
HARPER	Elspet	18	Marnoch	Marnoch	8	8
HARPER	George	47	Forgue ABD	Inverkeithny	3	2
HARPER	George	6	Forgue ABD	Inverkeithny	3	2
HARPER	George	2	Inverkeithny	Inverkeithny	2	9
HARPER	George	50	Marnoch	Marnoch	3	14
HARPER	Georgina	8	Marnoch	Marnoch	3	14
HARPER	Helen	22	Marnoch	Marnoch	6	1
HARPER	Helen	1	Forgue ABD	Inverkeithny	1	7
HARPER	Henry	14 days	Marnoch	Marnoch	1	8
HARPER	Hugh	7mths	Marnoch	Marnoch	3	14
HARPER	Isabel	11	Forgue ABD	Marnoch	1	2
HARPER	Isobel	50	Gamrie	Marnoch	8	7
HARPER	Isobel	74	Huntly ABD	Marnoch	3	2
HARPER	James	5	Marnoch	Marnoch	1	2
HARPER	James	8	Inverkeithny	Inverkeithny	1	6
HARPER	James	21	Auchterless ABD	Inverkeithny	2	9
HARPER	Jane	23	Huntly ABD	Marnoch	3	14
HARPER	Jane	31	Culsalmond ABD	Inverkeithny	1	7
HARPER	Janet	37	Fordyce	Marnoch	1	2
HARPER	Jean	2	Marnoch	Marnoch	1	2
HARPER	Jean	5	Gamrie	Marnoch	1	8
HARPER	Jean	73	Fyvie ABD	Marnoch	1	8
HARPER	John	36	Marnoch	Inverkeithny	1	7
HARPER	Lillie	44	Auchterless ABD	Inverkeithny	3	2
HARPER	Margaret	51	Marnoch	Marnoch	3	8
HARPER	Margaret	11	Marnoch	Marnoch	3	14
HARPER	Margaret	14	Gamrie	Marnoch	1	8
HARPER	Mary	2	Forglen	Forglen	2	6
HARPER	Mary	2mths	Inverkeithny	Inverkcithny	2	9
HARPER	Mary	36	Gamrie	Marnoch	1	8
HARPER	Mary	16	Gamrie	Marnoch	1	8
HARPER	Mary	17	Marnoch	Marnoch	6	7

SURNAME	CHR. NAME	AGE	BIRTH PLACE	CENSUS PARISH	BOOK	PG
HARPER	Peter	5mths	Inverkeithny	Inverkeithny	1	6
HARPER	Robert	44	Forgue ABD	Marnoch	1	2
HARPER	Robert	8	Marnoch	Marnoch	3	4
HARPER	William	60	Rothiemay	Marnoch	8	7
HARPER	William	14	Marnoch	Marnoch	4	8
HARPER	William	6	Inverkeithny	Inverkeithny	1	6
HARPER	William	5	Marnoch	Marnoch	3	14
HARRISON	Ann	21	Macduff	Marnoch	6	28
HARRISON	Helen	2	Macduff	Marnoch	6	28
HARVEY	Christina M.	8	Alves MOR	Forglen	2	8
HARVEY	Elizabeth A.	12	Jamaica	Forglen	2	8
HARVEY	Isaac Alexander	9mths	Forglen	Forglen	2	9
HARVEY	Isabella	31	St Andrews MOR	Forglen	2	8
HARVEY	James Charles	2	Forglen	Forglen	2	9
HARVEY	John	10	Jamaica	Forglen	2	8
HARVEY	Mary E.I.	4	Forglen	Forglen	2	8
HARVEY	William	51	Elgin MOR	Forglen	2	8
HARVEY	William James	6	Forglen	Forglen	2	8
HAY	Alexander	76	Inverkeithny	Marnoch	1	2
HAY	Alexander	12	Marnoch	Marnoch	4	18
HAY	Alexander	2	Marnoch	Marnoch	4	16
HAY	Alexander	2	Marnoch	Marnoch	4	12
HAY	Alexander	38	Marnoch	Forglen	3	5
HAY	Ann	10	Marnoch	Marnoch	9	4
HAY	Ann	38	Banff	Marnoch	4	16
HAY	Ann	5	Macduff	Forglen	3	5
HAY	Arthur	55	Monquhitter ABD	Marnoch	6	23
HAY	Charlotte	48	Rhynie ABD	Inverkeithny	2	2
HAY	Christian	14	Marnoch	Marnoch	9	4
HAY	Christian	50	Marnoch	Marnoch	9	4
HAY	Elspet	50	Alvah	Marnoch	8	9
HAY	George	16	Marnoch	Marnoch	9	4
HAY	George	17	Marnoch	Marnoch	4	1
HAY	James	53	Monquhitter ABD	Marnoch	3	5
HAY	James	5	Cairnie ABD	Marnoch	4	12
HAY	James	24	Marnoch	Marnoch	9	4
HAY	James	50	Marnoch	Marnoch	9	4
HAY	James	9mths	Marnoch	Marnoch	4	16
HAY	James	27	Marnoch	Marnoch	4	12
HAY	Janet	60	Ordiquhill	Marnoch	6	23
HAY	Janet	53	Forglen	Marnoch	6	17
HAY	Janet	24	Forgue ABD	Inverkeithny	2	6
HAY	Jean	19	Marnoch	Inverkeithny	2	8
HAY	Jessie	18	Marnoch	Marnoch	9	4
HAY	Jessie	17	Forgue ABD	Inverkeithny	1	4
HAY	John	35	Auchindoir ABD	Forglen	4	3
HAY	John	33	Marnoch	Marnoch	4	16
HAY	John	46	Bellie MOR	Marnoch	4	18
HAY	John	22	Marnoch	Marnoch	9	4
HAY	John	4	Marnoch	Marnoch	4	16
HAY	Margaret	82	Forgue ABD	Forglen	2	6
HAY	Margaret	26	Cairnie ABD	Marnoch	4	12
HAY	Margaret	50	Fyvie ABD	Marnoch	3	5
HAY	Margaret	42	Aberdeen ABD	Marnoch	4	18
HAY	Mary	70	Alvah	Marnoch	1	8
HAY	Robert	59	Clatt ABD	Marnoch	5	15
HAY	William	4	Marnoch	Marnoch	4	16
HAY	William	20	Marnoch	Marnoch	9	4
HAY	William	9	Marnoch	Forglen	3	5
HENDERSON	Alexander	4	Fyvie ABD	Inverkeithny	2	4
HENDERSON	Alexander	42	Kenmay ABD	Inverkeithny	2	4
HENDERSON	Ann	12	Logie Buchan ABD	Inverkeithny	2	4
HENDERSON	Christian	15	Culsalmond ABD	Inverkeithny	1	4
HENDERSON	Elizabeth	6	Echt ABD	Inverkeithny	2	4

SURNAME	CHR. NAME	AGE	BIRTH PLACE	CENSUS PARISH	BOOK	PG
HENDERSON	Elspet	60	Banff	Marnoch	6	28
HENDERSON	George	19	Marnoch	Forglen	4	1
HENDERSON	George	61	Aberdeen ABD	Marnoch	6	28
HENDERSON	Helen	11	Marnoch	Marnoch	4	10
HENDERSON	Helen	40	Lonmay ABD	Marnoch	4	10
HENDERSON	Isobel	57	Cabrach	Marnoch	3	18
HENDERSON	James	9	Marnoch	Marnoch	4	10
HENDERSON	James	38	King Edward ABD	Forglen	1	5
HENDERSON	John	62	Fraserburgh ABD	Inverkeithny	2	7
HENDERSON	John	27	Marnoch	Marnoch	6	28
HENDERSON	John	21	Wick CAI	Inverkeithny	1	10
HENDERSON	John	3	Inverkeithny	Inverkeithny	2	4
HENDERSON	Margaret	32	Aberdour ABD	Inverkeithny	2	4
HENDERSON	Theodore	7	Echt ABD	Inverkeithny	2	4
HENDERSON	William	1	Inverkeithny	Inverkeithny	2	5
HENDERSON	William	52	Monquhitter ABD	Marnoch	4	10
HENDRIE	Ann	14	Cairnie ABD	Marnoch	6	26
HENDRY	Charles	4	Marnoch	Marnoch	1	4
HENDRY	John N.	14	Inveravon	Marnoch	2	3
HENRY	Alexander	12	Marnoch	Marnoch	7	7
HENRY	Alexander	38	Rothiemay	Marnoch	6	5
HENRY	Ann	32	Marnoch	Marnoch	5	27
HENRY	Anne	30	Boyndie	Marnoch	7	9
HENRY	Barbara	25	Marnoch	Marnoch	6	5
HENRY	David	43	Fordoun KCD	Marnoch	5	27
HENRY	Elspet	61	Cairnie ABD	Marnoch	2	10
HENRY	Isabel C.	5	Marnoch	Marnoch	5	27
HENRY	James	1	Marnoch	Marnoch	6	5
HENRY	James	12	Marnoch	Marnoch	1	10
HENRY	James	23	Forglen	Marnoch	6	25
HENRY	Jane	26	Dyke MOR	Marnoch	7	4
HENRY	Jane	46	Marnoch	Marnoch	9	3
HENRY	Jane	4	Marnoch	Marnoch	6	5
HENRY	Jessie	24	Marnoch	Marnoch	6	29
HENRY	John	50	Turriff ABD	Marnoch	6	25
HENRY	John	61	Forglen	Forglen	1	8
HENRY	Margaret	21	Marnoch	Marnoch	6	26
HENRY	Margaret	41	Aberdeen ABD	Marnoch	5	27
HENRY	Thirzah	56	Marnoch	Marnoch	6	25
HENRY	William	4	Alvah	Marnoch	7	7
HENRY	William	64	Forglen	Forglen	1	8
HENRY	William	79	Boyndie	Marnoch	2	10
HENRY	William	27	Marnoch	Marnoch	2	10
HEPBURN	Elspet	33	Marnoch	Marnoch	7	12
HEPBURN	Elspet	14	Marnoch	Marnoch	7	12
HEPBURN	Francis	6	Marnoch	Marnoch	7	12
HEPBURN	George	11	Marnoch	Forglen	4	7
HEPBURN	James	55	Fraserburgh ABD	Forglen	4	7
HEPBURN	James	8	Marnoch	Marnoch	7	12
HEPBURN	Jane	4	Marnoch	Marnoch	7	12
HEPBURN	John	6mths	Marnoch	Marnoch	7	12
HEPBURN	Margaret	21	Aberdeen ABD	Forglen	2	9
HEPBURN	William	33	Aberdour ABD	Marnoch	7	12
HERD	Isabella	15	Forglen	Marnoch	8	7
HERD	James	13	King Edward ABD	Inverkeithny	1	1
HERD	Margaret	14	Huntly ABD	Marnoch	4	18
HETHERINGTON	Isabella	9	Canada	Forglen	2	9
HIND	Margaret	47	Forglen	Forglen	3	6
HINTON?	Margaret	39	Forglen	Marnoch	5	8
HIRD	Jean	77	Fordyce	Marnoch	9	5
HORN	Alexander	19	Marnoch	Marnoch	1	13
HORN	Alexander	39	Marnoch	Marnoch	1	9
HORN	Ann	84	Marnoch	Marnoch	1	12
HORN	Ann	18	Marnoch	Marnoch	6	29

SURNAME	CHR. NAME	AGE	BIRTH PLACE	CENSUS PARISH	BOOK	PG
HORN	Anne	25	Marnoch	Marnoch	6	27
HORN	Barbara	12	Marnoch	Marnoch	8	4
HORN	Elizabeth	67	Marnoch	Marnoch	5	22
HORN	George	44	Marnoch	Marnoch	1	9
HORN	George	49	Marnoch	Marnoch	5	5
HORN	George	17	Marnoch	Marnoch	8	9
HORN	George	53	Aberdeen-shire	Marnoch	6	29
HORN	George	15	Marnoch	Inverkeithny	2	10
HORN	George	3mths	Marnoch	Marnoch	6	29
HORN	Helen	31	Marnoch	Marnoch	3	1
HORN	Helen	41	Huntly ABD	Marnoch	6	29
HORN	Helen	56	Jamaica	Marnoch	3	1
HORN	Isabel	7	Marnoch	Marnoch	6	29
HORN	Isabella	31	Forgue ABD	Marnoch	5	5
HORN	James	1	Boyndie	Marnoch	5	26
HORN	James	2	Marnoch	Marnoch	6	29
HORN	Janet	63	Forgue ABD	Marnoch	6	12
HORN	John	11	Marnoch	Marnoch	6	29
HORN	John	22	Marnoch	Marnoch	3	1
HORN	William	5	Marnoch	Marnoch	6	29
HORN	William	15	Marnoch	Inverkeithny	3	10
HORNE	Elizie	12	Marnoch	Marnoch	7	9
HORNE	Jean	19	Rothiemay	Marnoch	8	3
HOSIE	Anne	1	Marnoch	Marnoch	9	5
HOSIE	James	4	Alvah	Marnoch	9	5
HOSIE	James	28	Inverurie ABD	Marnoch	9	5
HOSIE	Margaret	35	Alvah	Marnoch	9	5
HOSIE	Margaret	3mths	Marnoch	Marnoch	9	5
HOULTON	Thomas	1	Marnoch	Forglen	3	6
HOWAT	George	28	Inverkeithny	Inverkeithny	1	6
HOWEL	Robert	18	Ordiquhill	Inverkeithny	1	1
HOWIE	Ann	40	Grange	Marnoch	7	6
HOWIE	Catherine	13	King Edward ABD	Forglen	1	3
HOWIE	Elizabeth	73	New York	Marnoch	7	15
HOWIE	George	5	Rothiemay	Marnoch	7	6
HOWIE	George	36	Keith	Marnoch	7	6
HOWIE	James	10	Rothiemay	Marnoch	7	6
HOWIE	James	11	King Edward ABD	Forglen	1	3
HOWIE	Jessie	19	Rathven	Forglen	1	3
HOWIE	Margaret	15	Grange	Inverkeithny	2	10
HOWIE	Robert	48	Forgue ABD	Forglen	1	3
HOWIT	Ann	58	Marnoch	Marnoch	3	5
HUNTER	Mary	13	Auchindoir ABD	Marnoch	3	18
HUTCHEON	Christian	3	Marnoch	Marnoch	3	3
HUTCHEON	George	44	Turriff ABD	Marnoch	3	2
HUTCHEON	Helen	11mths	Marnoch	Marnoch	9	8
HUTCHEON	Isabella	50	Forgue ABD	Inverkeithny	1	3
HUTCHEON	Isabella	44	Rothiemay	Marnoch	3	2
HUTCHEON	Isobel	16	Marnoch	Marnoch	3	3
HUTCHEON	James	19	Marnoch	Forglen	2	9
HUTCHEON	James	26	Forgue ABD	Inverkeithny	1	3
HUTCHEON	Jean	14	Inverkeithny	Inverkeithny	1	3
HUTCHEON	Jean	12	Marnoch	Marnoch	3	3
HUTCHEON	Margaret	6	Marnoch	Marnoch	3	3
HUTCHEON	Mary	18	Marnoch	Marnoch	3	2
HUTCHEON	Robert	8	Marnoch	Marnoch	3	3
HUTCHEON	William	53	Rayne ABD	Inverkeithny	1	3
HUTCHISON	Ann	17	Banff	Marnoch	6	12
Hay	Geo	68	Clatt ABD	Forglen	3	5
Hay	Geo	11	Marnoch	Forglen	3	5
Hay	Isabella	13	Marnoch	Forglen	3	5
IMLACH	Ann	55	Boyndie	Marnoch	5	8
IMLACH	Catheirne	78	Marnoch	Marnoch	6	15
IMLACH	Duncan	5	Rothiemay	Marnoch	7	14

SURNAME	CHR. NAME	AGE	BIRTH PLACE	CENSUS PARISH	BOOK	PG
IMLACH	Isabella	11	Rathven	Marnoch	7	13
IMLACH	James	45	Marnoch	Marnoch	7	13
IMLACH	Janet	38	Rathven	Marnoch	7	13
IMLACH	Janet	78	Marnoch	Marnoch	6	13
IMLACH	Margaret	9mths	Marnoch	Marnoch	7	14
IMLACH	William	3	Rothiemay	Marnoch	7	14
INGELS	Alexander	14	Forgue ABD	Marnoch	4	2
INGLIS	Alexander	30	Marnoch	Marnoch	5	19
INGLIS	Elizabeth	35	Marnoch	Marnoch	6	22
INGLIS	Elspet	19	Marnoch	Marnoch	5	19
INGLIS	George	29	Marnoch	Inverkeithny	2	13
INGLIS	Helen	2	Marnoch	Marnoch	6	22
INGLIS	James	68	Fordyce	Marnoch	5	19
INGLIS	James	39	Marnoch	Marnoch	6	22
INGLIS	Mary	16	Forgue ABD	Inverkeithny	1	11
INGRAM	Christian	35	Marnoch	Marnoch	7	10
INGRAM	Eliza	17	Forgue ABD	Marnoch	3	18
INGRAM	Elspet	4	Marnoch	Marnoch	7	11
INGRAM	George	37	Forgue ABD	Marnoch	6	6
INGRAM	James	7	Marnoch	Marnoch	3	16
INGRAM	James	10	Marnoch	Marnoch	7	10
INGRAM	Jane	25	Rothiemay	Marnoch	3	16
INGRAM	Jane	4	Marnoch	Marnoch	3	16
INGRAM	Janet	62	Gamrie	Marnoch	1	3
INGRAM	Lida	26	Marnoch	Marnoch	1	3
INGRAM	Margaret	1	Marnoch	Marnoch	3	16
INGRAM	Sarah	7	Marnoch	Marnoch	7	11
INGRAM	William	34	Marnoch	Marnoch	3	16
INGRAM	William	2	Forgue ABD	Marnoch	3	6
INGRAM	William	61	Rothiemay	Marnoch	1	3
INGRAM	William	35	Forgue ABD	Marnoch	7	10
INNES	Alexander	13	Marnoch	Marnoch	4	11
INNES	Alexander	1	Marnoch	Marnoch	5	21
INNES	Alexander	5	Marnoch	Marnoch	3	18
INNES	Alexander	78	Marnoch	Marnoch	4	11
INNES	Alexander	28	Marnoch	Marnoch	5	21
INNES	Alexander	7	Marnoch	Marnoch	6	14
INNES	Elizabeth	6	Inveravon	Marnoch	2	6
INNES	Elizabeth O.Rose	40	Marnoch	Marnoch	8	7
INNES	Elspet	69	Marnoch	Marnoch	4	9
INNES	George	3	Marnoch	Marnoch	6	14
INNES	Hariot	34	Inveravon	Marnoch	2	6
INNES	Isobel	61	Marnoch	Marnoch	4	15
INNES	James	35	Marnoch	Marnoch	3	17
INNES	James	11	Marnoch	Marnoch	3	3
INNES	James	28	Marnoch	Marnoch	4	15
INNES	James	1	Marnoch	Marnoch	3	18
INNES	James	9	Marnoch	Marnoch	6	14
INNES	Jane	29	Marnoch	Marnoch	5	21
INNES	Jane	7	Marnoch	Marnoch	3	18
INNES	Jane	43	Cairnie ABD	Marnoch	6	14
INNES	Janet	71	Fordyce	Marnoch	4	11
INNES	Jean	7	Marnoch	Marnoch	5	21
INNES	John	4mths	Marnoch	Marnoch	2	6
INNES	John	2	Marnoch	Marnoch	6	14
INNES	John	50	Marnoch	Marnoch	6	14
INNES	Margaret	10	Marnoch	Marnoch	3	18
INNES	Margaret	4	Inveravon	Marnoch	2	6
INNES	Margaret	32	Marnoch	Marnoch	3	17
INNES	Mary	55	Marnoch	Marnoch	1	8
INNES	Mary	38	Marnoch	Marnoch	4	11
INNES	Mary	5	Marnoch	Marnoch	3	3
INNES	Mary	39	Rothiemay	Marnoch	3	3
INNES	Mary	5	Marnoch	Marnoch	6	15

SURNAME	CHR. NAME	AGE	BIRTH PLACE	CENSUS PARISH	BOOK	PG
INNES	Patrick Rose	46	Marnoch	Marnoch	8	7
INNES	Robert	10	Marnoch	Marnoch	3	3
INNES	Susie	33	Marnoch	Marnoch	4	11
INNES	Thomas	11	Marnoch	Marnoch	6	14
INNES	William	31	Inveravon	Marnoch	2	6
INNES	William	43	Marnoch	Marnoch	3	3
INNES	William	14	Marnoch	Inverkeithny	1	6
IRONSIDE	Ann	2	Inverkeithny	Inverkeithny	2	2
IRONSIDE	Elizabeth	6mths	Inverkeithny	Inverkeithny	2	2
IRONSIDE	Isabella	34	Keith	Inverkeithny	2	2
IRONSIDE	Isabella	5	Inverkeithny	Inverkeithny	2	2
IRONSIDE	Jean	8mths	Marnoch	Marnoch	6	29
IRONSIDE	Jean	8	Inverkeithny	Inverkeithny	2	2
IRONSIDE	Robert	23	Peterhead ABD	Inverkeithny	3	10
IRONSIDE	William	6	Inverkeithny	Inverkeithny	2	2
IRONSIDE	William	42	King Edward ABD	Inverkeithny	2	2
Inglis	Geo	6	Forglen	Forglen	2	11
Inglis	Isabel	78	Marnoch	Forglen	4	9
Inglis	Margt	38	Forglen	Forglen	2	11
Inglis	Wm	43	Fordyce	Forglen	2	11
Inglis	Wm	16	Forglen	Forglen	2	11
Inglis	Wm	80	Fordyce	Forglen	4	9
Innes	Eliz.	22	Prenmay ABD	Forglen	3	3
Innes	Geo	1	Forglen	Forglen	3	3
Innes	Jn	16	Marnoch	Forglen	2	5
Innes	Jn	31	Rayne ABD	Forglen	3	3
Innes	Jn	22	Inveravon	Forglen	2	4
Innes	Margt	11	Macduff	Forglen	2	7
Innes	Mary Ann	27	Rayne ABD	Forglen	3	3
Ironside	Jn	21	King Edward ABD	Forglen	4	3
JAMIESON	Alison	2	Marnoch	Marnoch	6	3
JAMIESON	Ann	4	Marnoch	Marnoch	6	3
JAMIESON	David	25	New Deer ABD	Marnoch	8	2
JAMIESON	James	9mths	Marnoch	Marnoch	8	11
JAMIESON	Jean	27	Marnoch	Marnoch	6	16
JAMIESON	Jessie	1mth	Marnoch	Marnoch	6	3
JAMIESON	John	2	Marnoch	Marnoch	6	16
JAMIESON	Joseph	27	Aberdeen ABD	Marnoch	6	16
JAMIESON	Mary	36	Ordiquhill	Marnoch	6	3
JAMIESON	Mary	2	Marnoch	Marnoch	6	3
JAMIESON	Susan	4	Marnoch	Marnoch	6	16
JAMIESON	Thomas	41	Alvah	Marnoch	6	27
JESSIMAN	Robert	31	Huntly ABD	Inverkeithny	1	9
JOASS	Helen	61	Megvie ABD	Marnoch	5	16
JOASS	Margaret	58	Alvah	Marnoch	5	24
JOHNSTON	Alexander	18	Marnoch	Marnoch	1	14
JOHNSTON	Alexander	3mths	Marnoch	Marnoch	5	11
JOHNSTON	Alexander	43	Cairnie ABD	Marnoch	5	11
JOHNSTON	Alexander	73	Marnoch	Marnoch	6	16
JOHNSTON	Ann	36	Marnoch	Marnoch	5	3
JOHNSTON	David	11	Marnoch	Marnoch	6	21
JOHNSTON	Elspet	67	Marnoch	Marnoch	5	12
JOHNSTON	George	2	Marnoch	Marnoch	6	20
JOHNSTON	Helen	26	Forglen	Marnoch	5	1
JOHNSTON	Helen	48	Marnoch	Marnoch	6	21
JOHNSTON	Helen	76	Marnoch	Marnoch	6	19
JOHNSTON	Helen	9	Marnoch	Marnoch	6	21
JOHNSTON	Jane	13	Marnoch	Marnoch	5	3
JOHNSTON	Jean	6	Marnoch	Marnoch	6	20
JOHNSTON	Jessie	4	Marnoch	Marnoch	5	11
JOHNSTON	Joseph	14	Marnoch	Marnoch	4	1
JOHNSTON	Joseph	24	Marnoch	Marnoch	9	6
JOHNSTON	Margaret	3	Marnoch	Marnoch	5	11
JOHNSTON	Margaret	4	Marnoch	Marnoch	6	20

SURNAME	CHR. NAME	AGE	BIRTH PLACE	CENSUS PARISH	BOOK	PG
JOHNSTON	Mary	36	Forgue ABD	Marnoch	6	20
JOHNSTON	William	24	Marnoch	Marnoch	5	5
JOSS	Mary	59	Forgue ABD	Marnoch	7	5
JOSS	Mary	27	Marnoch	Marnoch	6	15
JOSS?	female	9mths	Marnoch	Marnoch	6	15
Jamieson	Alex	7	Forglen	Forglen	4	6
Jamieson	Andrew	30	Turriff ABD	Forglen	2	10
Jamieson	Geo	20	Forglen	Forglen	4	7
Jamieson	Geo	46	Marnoch	Forglen	4	6
Jamieson	James	17	Forglen	Forglen	4	7
Jamieson	Jane	11	Forglen	Forglen	4	7
Jamieson	Jane	46	Forglen	Forglen	4	7
Jamieson	Jn	9	Forglen	Forglen	4	7
Jamieson	Jn	5	Forglen	Forglen	4	6
Jamieson	Margt	80	Marnoch	Forglen	4	6
Jamieson	Margt	3	Forglen	Forglen	4	6
Jamieson	Margt	43	King Edward ABD	Forglen	4	6
Jamieson	Wm	14	Forglen	Forglen	4	7
Jamieson	Wm	50	Marnoch	Forglen	4	7
Jenkins	Geo	20	Banff	Forglen	1	9
Johnston	Alex	58	Boyndie	Forglen	4	8
Johnston	Alex	20	Ordiquhill	Forglen	1	8
Johnston	Ann	19	Banff	Forglen	1	5
Johnston	Eliz.	34	Banff	Forglen	4	8
Johnston	Francis	15	Alvah	Forglen	4	8
Johnston	Jane	56	Banff	Forglen	4	8
Johnston	Jn	15	Alvah	Forglen	4	8
Johnston	Margt	17	Cummineston ABD	Forglen	1	3
Joiner	Jn	3mths	Forglen	Forglen	1	2
Joiner	Jn	32	Banff	Forglen	1	2
Joiner	Mary	22	Forglen	Forglen	1	2
Joiner	Thomas	63	Boyndie	Forglen	1	2
KEITH	George	2	Marnoch	Marnoch	6	29
KEITH	Jean	66	Turriff ABD	Marnoch	5	4
KEITH	William	10	Longside ABD	Marnoch	6	11
KELLY?	Mary	66	Auchterless ABD	Marnoch	5	22
KELMAN	Alexander	11	Kenmay ABD	Marnoch	5	15
KELMAN	Alexander	29	Fordyce	Inverkeithny	2	7
KELMAN	Alexander	57	Auchterless ABD	Marnoch	6	12
KELMAN	Elizabeth	76	Clatt ABD	Marnoch	6	12
KELMAN	Elspet	22	Marnoch	Marnoch	5	15
KELMAN	George	10	Marnoch	Marnoch	5	15
KELMAN	James	4	Dyke MOR	Marnoch	7	4
KELMAN	Janet	20	Fordyce	Marnoch	4	5
KELMAN	Jean	12	Marnoch	Marnoch	5	15
KELMAN	John	16	Marnoch	Marnoch	5	15
KELMAN	Mary	24	Marnoch	Marnoch	6	12
KELMAN	Mary	53	Fordyce	Marnoch	5	15
KELMAN	William	51	Alvah	Marnoch	7	7
KELMAN	William	28	Marnoch	Marnoch	5	15
KERR	Mary	59	Huntly ABD	Marnoch	3	5
KIDD	James	24	Inverkeithny	Inverkeithny	1	6
KIDD	Jessie	21	King Edward ABD	Marnoch	3	15
KIDD	John	33	Gamrie	Marnoch	8	5
KIDD	Thomas	40	Tullyallan PER	Marnoch	3	2
KING	Alexander	25	Cairnie ABD	Marnoch	8	2
KINNAIRD	Alexander	66	Keith	Marnoch	5	22
KINNAIRD	James	19	Marnoch	Marnoch	5	23
KINNAIRD	Janet	62	Rothiemay	Marnoch	5	22
KINNAIRD	Jessie	26	Marnoch	Marnoch	5	22
KNIGHT	John	38	Huntly ABD	Marnoch	9	10
KNIGHT	Margaret	33	Huntly ABD	Marnoch	9	10
KNIGHT	Margaret A.	5	Huntly ABD	Marnoch	9	10
Keith	Elspet	12	Longside ABD	Forglen	4	4

SURNAME	CHR. NAME	AGE	BIRTH PLACE	CENSUS PARISH	BOOK	PG
Kelman	Helen	24	Forglen	Forglen	2	4
Kelman	James	35	Gamrie	Forglen	1	3
King	Agnes	18	Forglen	Forglen	1	4
King	Alex	73	Forglen	Forglen	1	4
King	Alex	29	Forglen	Forglen	1	4
King	Elspet	20	Forglen	Forglen	1	4
King	Janet	13	Forglen	Forglen	1	3
King	Jean	26	Forglen	Forglen	1	4
King	Sarah	63	Gamrie	Forglen	1	4
King	Wm	24	Forglen	Forglen	1	4
King	Wm	25	Cairnie	Forglen	2	7
LAMB	John	35	Daviot ABD	Inverkeithny	2	5
LAMONT	Robert	19	Turriff ABD	Marnoch	3	13
LARGUE	Christian	30	Inverkeithny	Inverkeithny	1	1
LARGUE	Elspet	10mths	Inverkeithny	Inverkeithny	1	12
LARGUE	George	83	Inverkeithny	Inverkeithny	1	1
LARGUE	George	1	Inverkeithny	Inverkeithny	1	1
LARGUE	Helen	68	Marnoch	Inverkeithny	1	1
LARGUE	James	5mths	Inverkeithny	Inverkeithny	1	1
LARGUE	James I.C.	4	Forgue ABD	Inverkeithny	1	12
LARGUE	Mary	32	Auchterless ABD	Inverkeithny	1	12
LARGUE	Mary	8	Forgue ABD	Inverkeithny	1	12
LARGUE	Robert J.	33	Inverkeithny	Inverkeithny	1	1
LARGUE	William	33	Forgue ABD	Inverkeithny	1	12
LATHER	James	1	Marnoch	Marnoch	6	12
LATHER	James	24	Huntly ABD	Marnoch	6	20
LAUDER	Alexander	8	Marnoch	Marnoch	6	4
LAUDER	Elizabeth	5	Marnoch	Marnoch	6	4
LAUDER	James	47	Marnoch	Marnoch	6	4
LAUDER	James	22	Fordyce	Marnoch	2	8
LAUDER	Nancy A.	3mths	Marnoch	Marnoch	6	4
LAUDER	William	3	Marnoch	Marnoch	6	4
LAWRANCE	Janet	68	Fordyce	Marnoch	7	11
LAWRENCE	George	16	Culsalmond ABD	Inverkeithny	2	12
LAWRENCE	Mary	15	Rothiemay	Marnoch	6	8
LAWSON	Alexander	10mths	Inverkeithny	Inverkeithny	1	5
LAWSON	Jemima	3	Marnoch	Marnoch	6	7
LEADINGHAM	Ann	6	Daviot ABD	Marnoch	4	5
LEADINGHAM	John	46	Chapel of Garioch ABD	Marnoch	4	5
LEADINGHAM	John	5	Daviot ABD	Marnoch	4	5
LEADINGHAM	Mary	38	Daviot ABD	Marnoch	4	5
LEDINGHAM	Alexander	20	Turriff ABD	Inverkeithny	3	15
LEDINGHAM	Mary	23	Culsalmond ABD	Inverkeithny	1	1
LEGGAT	Catherine	29	Marnoch	Marnoch	9	8
LEGGAT	Elspet	10	Forglen	Marnoch	9	11
LEGGAT	Helen	60	Marnoch	Marnoch	9	8
LEGGAT	James	62	Forglen	Marnoch	9	8
LEGGAT	John	40	Marnoch	Marnoch	9	10
LEGGAT	John	14	Forglen	Marnoch	9	10
LEGGAT	Margaret	6	Marnoch	Marnoch	9	11
LEGGAT	Rachel	35	Forglen	Marnoch	9	10
LEGGAT	William	8	Forglen	Marnoch	9	11
LEITH	Alexander	84	Clatt ABD	Marnoch	3	1
LEITH	Alexander	2	Marnoch	Marnoch	3	15
LEITH	Anne	15	Marnoch	Marnoch	3	15
LEITH	Elizabeth	80	Leslie ABD	Marnoch	3	1
LEITH	George	35	Leslie ABD	Marnoch	3	1
LEITH	George	7	Marnoch	Marnoch	3	15
LEITH	Jane	4mths	Marnoch	Marnoch	3	15
LEITH	Lawrance	13	Marnoch	Marnoch	7	3
LEITH	Lawrence	44	Marnoch	Marnoch	3	15
LEITH	Mary	37	Marnoch	Marnoch	3	15
LEITH	William	4	Marnoch	Marnoch	3	15
LEITH	William	38	Leslie ABD	Marnoch	3	1

SURNAME	CHR. NAME	AGE	BIRTH PLACE	CENSUS PARISH	BOOK	PG
LEMMON?	Elspet	23	Grange	Inverkeithny	3	4
LEMMOND	Elspet	50	Grange	Marnoch	6	17
LEMMOND	Helen	16	Grange	Marnoch	6	17
LEMMOND	James	20mths	Fordyce	Marnoch	6	17
LEMON	William	21	Forgue ABD	Marnoch	1	1
LESLIE	Alexander	45	Marnoch	Marnoch	7	9
LESLIE	Findlater	4mths	Marnoch	Marnoch	3	17
LESLIE	Helen	11	Keith	Marnoch	7	9
LESLIE	James	7	Marnoch	Marnoch	7	9
LESLIE	James	22	Marnoch	Marnoch	8	12
LESLIE	John	3	Marnoch	Marnoch	7	9
LESLIE	Nanny	33	Banff	Marnoch	7	9
LESLIE	Robert	7	Alvah	Marnoch	5	21
LISTER	Ann	40	Elgin MOR	Marnoch	5	16
LITTLEJOHN	Alexander	25	Aberdeenshire	Inverkeithny	3	5
LITTLEJOHN	Isobel	21	Old Machar ABD	Marnoch	1	10
LOBBAN	Alexander	10mths	Marnoch	Marnoch	1	14
LOBBAN	Alexander	32	Boyndie	Marnoch	1	14
LOBBAN	Christian	72	Alvah	Marnoch	2	12
LOBBAN	Christian	37	Inverkeithny	Inverkeithny	2	13
LOBBAN	Elspet	16	Marnoch	Marnoch	6	16
LOBBAN	Helen	34	Turriff ABD	Marnoch	1	14
LOBBAN	Isabella	8	Marnoch	Marnoch	6	16
LOBBAN	Isabella	40	Marnoch	Marnoch	6	16
LOBBAN	James	8	Turriff ABD	Marnoch	1	14
LOBBAN	James	10	Marnoch	Marnoch	6	16
LOBBAN	James	64	Rothiemay	Marnoch	2	12
LOBBAN	Jane	3	Marnoch	Marnoch	1	14
LOBBAN	Jane	12	Inverkeithny	Marnoch	2	12
LOBBAN	Jane	2	Marnoch	Marnoch	6	16
LOBBAN	Jean	55	Rathven	Marnoch	6	4
LOBBAN	John	6	Marnoch	Marnoch	6	16
LOBBAN	Joseph	5	Marnoch	Marnoch	6	16
LOBBAN	Margaret	58	Marnoch	Marnoch	5	22
LOBBAN	Mary	5	Inverkeithny	Inverkeithny	2	6
LOBBAN	Mary	1	Marnoch	Marnoch	6	16
LOBBAN	Mary	29	Inverkeithny	Inverkeithny	2	6
LOBBAN	Mary	60	Marnoch	Marnoch	5	7
LOBBAN	William	1	Inverkeithny	Inverkeithny	2	6
LORIMER	David	24	Aberdeen ABD	Marnoch	5	1
LORIMER	Eliza	14	Marnoch	Marnoch	6	19
LORIMER	Helen	22	Marnoch	Marnoch	6	18
LORIMER	Helen	46	Marnoch	Marnoch	6	18
LORIMER	Jane	64	Forglen	Marnoch	6	4
LORIMER	Jane	19	Marnoch	Marnoch	6	18
LORIMER	Jessie	18mths	Marnoch	Marnoch	6	19
LORIMER	John	52	Forglen	Marnoch	6	18
LORIMER	William	27	Aberdeen ABD	Marnoch	5	1
LOW	Ann	35	Marnoch	Marnoch	5	2
LOW	Elizabeth	18	Forgue ABD	Inverkeithny	1	7
LYON	Alexander	64	Grange	Marnoch	2	12
LYON	Alexander	17	Marnoch	Marnoch	4	14
LYON	Andrew	24	Marnoch	Marnoch	7	14
LYON	Anne	14	Marnoch	Marnoch	7	6
LYON	Charlotte B.	2	Marnoch	Marnoch	2	6
LYON	Elizabeth	59	Banff	Marnoch	7	14
LYON	Elizabeth	2	Marnoch	Marnoch	7	6
LYON	Elspet	35	Grange	Marnoch	2	6
LYON	Isabel	70	Marnoch	Marnoch	1	2
LYON	Isabella	22	Cairnie ABD	Marnoch	2	7
LYON	Isabella	6	Marnoch	Marnoch	7	6
LYON	Isabella	17	Marnoch	Marnoch	2	12
LYON	Isobel	56	Cairnie ABD	Marnoch	2	10
LYON	James	23	Garnge	Marnoch	2	7

SURNAME	CHR. NAME	AGE	BIRTH PLACE	CENSUS PARISH	BOOK	PG
LYON	James	29	Marnoch	Marnoch	7	14
LYON	James	13	Marnoch	Marnoch	7	6
LYON	James	51	Marnoch	Marnoch	2	6
LYON	James	62	Grange	Marnoch	7	6
LYON	James	33	Inverkeithny	Inverkeithny	2	6
LYON	James	21	Huntly ABD	Inverkeithny	1	2
LYON	James M.	1	Inverkeithny	Inverkeithny	2	6
LYON	Jane	4	Marnoch	Marnoch	9	4
LYON	Jane	17	Marnoch	Marnoch	2	10
LYON	Janet	57	Fordyce	Marnoch	2	6
LYON	John	1mth	Inverkeithny	Inverkeithny	2	6
LYON	John	68	Marnoch	Marnoch	5	23
LYON	John	21	Methlick ABD	Inverkeithny	3	12
LYON	John	27	Marnoch	Marnoch	6	8
LYON	John	10	Marnoch	Marnoch	7	6
LYON	Margaret	45	Cairnie ABD	Marnoch	7	6
LYON	William	18	Marnoch	Marnoch	7	6
LYON	William	1mth	Inverkeithny	Inverkeithny	1	8
LYON	William	20	Marnoch	Marnoch	6	9
LYON	William	21	Grange	Marnoch	2	6
LYON	William	59	Marnoch	Marnoch	2	10
LYON	William	53	Marnoch	Marnoch	7	14
LYON	William	1	Cairnie ABD	Marnoch	2	7
LYON	female	1 week	Marnoch	Marnoch	6	8
Laing	Ann	9	New Deer ABD	Forglen	1	1
Laing	Jane	14	New Deer ABD	Forglen	1	1
Laing	Mary	43	Methlick ABD	Forglen	1	1
Laing	Mary	12	New Deer ABD	Forglen	1	1
Laing	Rob	47	Old Deer ABD	Forglen	1	1
Lammont	Geo	15	Slains ABD	Forglen	4	4
Lamond	Jn	25	Snizort INV	Forglen	4	7
Lamont	Ann	48	Birse ABD	Forglen	1	2
Lamont	Eliz	8	Forglen	Forglen	1	2
Lamont	Elspet	10	Forglen	Forglen	1	2
Lamont	Geo	14	Forglen	Forglen	1	8
Lamont	James	55	Braemar ABD	Forglen	1	2
Lamont	Jessie	1	Forglen	Forglen	1	2
Lamont	Mary	4	Forglen	Forglen	1	2
Ledingham	Alex	24	Insch ABD	Forglen	3	8
Leggat	Jn	16	King Edward ABD	Forglen	1	4
Leslie	James	6	Forglen	Forglen	1	8
Leslie	James	56	Forglen	Forglen	1	8
Leslie	Jane	4	Forgue ABD	Forglen	4	1
Leslie	Jane	45	Forglen	Forglen	1	8
Leslie	Margt	45	Marnoch	Forglen	1	8
Leslie	Margt	8	Forglen	Forglen	1	8
Leslie	Margt	53	Forglen	Forglen	2	4
Leslie	Mary	43	Alvah	Forglen	4	5
Linton	Eliz.	21	Peterhead ABD	Forglen	1	5
Loban	Christian	35	Forglen	Forglen	4	3
Loban	Isabella	60	Forgue ABD	Forglen	4	3
Loban	Isabella	28	Forglen	Forglen	4	3
Loban	James	65	Fordyce	Forglen	4	3
Loban	Jn	26	Forglen	Forglen	4	3
Lobban	Isabella	20	Rothiemay	Forglen	3	8
Lobban	Margt	78	Fordyce	Forglen	2	10
Lyon	Geo	21	Grange	Forglen	4	9
Lyon	James	55	Fordyce	Forglen	4	3
Lyon	Jane	45	Marnoch	Forglen	4	3
Lyon	Margt	79	Alvah	Forglen	4	5
Lyon	Robert	11	Forglen	Forglen	4	3
MACADAM	Alexander	33	Maybole AYR	Inverkeithny	1	2
MACADAM	Margaret	20	Culsalmond ABD	Forglen	4	9
MACANDREW	Helen	52	Inverkeithny	Inverkeithny	1	10

SURNAME	CHR. NAME	AGE	BIRTH PLACE	CENSUS PARISH	BOOK	PG
MACANDREW	William	50	Crathie ABD	Inverkeithny	1	10
MACARTHUR	Eliza	30	Edinburgh MLN	Marnoch	4	15
MACARTHUR	George	20	Ireland	Marnoch	8	6
MACARTHUR	Jane	24	Huntly ABD	Marnoch	9	10
MACARTHUR	Jean	70	Mortlach	Marnoch	4	15
MACARTHUR	Jean	38	Ayr AYR	Marnoch	4	15
MACARTHUR	Peter	84	Calder NAI	Marnoch	4	15
MACARTHUR	William	16	Drumblade ABD	Marnoch	9	10
MACBAIN	Betsy	32	Boyndie	Marnoch	4	14
MACBAIN	Isabel	12	Huntly ABD	Marnoch	6	27
MACBAIN	James	1	Marnoch	Marnoch	4	14
MACBAIN	Jane	40	Aberlour ABD (?)	Marnoch	6	27
MACBAIN	John	6	Boyndie	Marnoch	4	14
MACBAIN	Peter	7	Marnoch	Marnoch	6	27
MACBAIN	William	5	Marnoch	Marnoch	6	27
MACBAIN	William	34	Fordyce	Marnoch	4	14
MACBAINB	Margaret	24	Fordyce	Forglen	2	7
MACCARTY	Jean	22	Aberdour ABD	Marnoch	8	12
MACCOMBIE	James	57	Rayne ABD	Inverkeithny	2	8
MACCOMBIE	Jean	52	Inverkeithny	Inverkeithny	2	8
MACCOMBIE	John	22	Rayne ABD	Inverkeithny	2	8
MACCOMBIE	William	14	Fordyce	Marnoch	7	8
MACCRAE	Peter	9	Marnoch	Marnoch	6	14
MACDERMOT	Mathew	35	Cavan IRL	Marnoch	5	2
MACDONALD	Alexander	73	Inverness INV	Inverkeithny	2	15
MACDONALD	Alexander	61	Inverness-shire	Marnoch	7	2
MACDONALD	Alexander	26	Marnoch	Marnoch	7	2
MACDONALD	Alexander	27	Marnoch	Marnoch	7	3
MACDONALD	Alexander	15	Rothes MOR	Marnoch	3	5
MACDONALD	Ann	17	Marnoch	Marnoch	7	2
MACDONALD	Catherine	37	Marnoch	Marnoch	6	25
MACDONALD	Elizabeth	8	Marnoch	Marnoch	7	2
MACDONALD	Elspet	50	Speymouth MOR	Marnoch	3	5
MACDONALD	Elspet	7	Turriff ABD	Marnoch	3	5
MACDONALD	Eslept	50	Elgin MOR	Marnoch	3	13
MACDONALD	Helen	10	Rothes MOR	Marnoch	3	5
MACDONALD	Henry	36	King Edward ABD	Inverkeithny	1	7
MACDONALD	Isobel	12	Rothes MOR	Marnoch	3	5
MACDONALD	James	14	Rothes MOR	Marnoch	3	5
MACDONALD	James	16	Marnoch	Marnoch	7	2
MACDONALD	Jane	19	Marnoch	Marnoch	7	2
MACDONALD	John	18	Rothes MOR	Marnoch	3	5
MACDONALD	John	39	Speymouth MOR	Marnoch	3	5
MACDONALD	John	21	Marnoch	Marnoch	7	2
MACDONALD	John	20	Boyndie	Marnoch	2	2
MACDONALD	Lockhart	21	Inverness INV	Inverkeithny	1	3
MACDONALD	Margaret	3	Marnoch	Marnoch	7	3
MACDONALD	Mary	60	Inverness-shire	Marnoch	7	2
MACDONALD	Mary	1	Marnoch	Marnoch	7	3
MACEWAN	james	20	Glass ABD	Marnoch	8	6
MACEWEN	John	32	Carlisle CUL	Forglen	2	3
MACFADDEN	Jane	27	Ireland	Marnoch	5	20
MACGLASHAN	Mary	25	Ardclach NAI	Inverkeithny	2	1
MACGREGOR	Agnes	2	Marnoch	Marnoch	6	3
MACGREGOR	John	9	Marnoch	Marnoch	6	3
MACGREGOR	Margaret	5	Marnoch	Marnoch	6	3
MACGREGOR	Mary	8	Marnoch	Marnoch	6	3
MACGREGOR	Mary	45	Marnoch	Marnoch	6	3
MACGRIGOR	Helen	18	Marnoch	Marnoch	4	18
MACGRIGOR	Mary	14	Marnoch	Marnoch	5	7
MACGUIRE	James	21	Roscommon IRL	Inverkeithny	1	3
MACHARDIE	Mary	14	Marnoch	Marnoch	2	10
MACHARDY	Alexander	44	Banff	Marnoch	4	9
MACHARDY	Alexander	4	Forglen	Forglen	3	2

SURNAME	CHR. NAME	AGE	BIRTH PLACE	CENSUS PARISH	BOOK	PG
MACHARDY	Catherine	6	Marnoch	Marnoch	4	9
MACHARDY	George	36	Forglen	Forglen	2	4
MACHARDY	Isabella	33	Forglen	Forglen	2	4
MACHARDY	James	39	Forglen	Forglen	3	2
MACHARDY	James	11	Forglen	Forglen	3	2
MACHARDY	Janet	40	Marnoch	Marnoch	4	9
MACHARDY	Janet	77	Deskford	Forglen	2	4
MACHARDY	Jessie	10	Marnoch	Marnoch	4	9
MACHARDY	John	6	Forglen	Forglen	3	2
MACHARDY	John	46	Banff	Marnoch	4	9
MACHARDY	Margaret	34	Forglen	Forglen	3	2
MACHARDY	Mary	42	Banff	Forglen	2	4
MACHARDY	William	7	Forglen	Forglen	3	2
MACHATTIE	Helen	19	Fordyce	Marnoch	2	12
MACINTOSH	Alexander	6	Marnoch	Marnoch	6	15
MACINTOSH	Alexander	26	Grange	Marnoch	8	12
MACINTOSH	Alexander	70	Marnoch	Marnoch	3	17
MACINTOSH	Alexander	6	Inverkeithny	Inverkeithny	1	11
MACINTOSH	Ann	12	Marnoch	Marnoch	2	14
MACINTOSH	Ann	51	Marnoch	Marnoch	6	15
MACINTOSH	Ann	1	Inverkeithny	Inverkeithny	1	11
MACINTOSH	Ann	18	Alvah	Inverkeithny	2	5
MACINTOSH	Anne	15	Banff town	Marnoch	7	8
MACINTOSH	Bryce	50	Cawdor NAI	Inverkeithny	2	6
MACINTOSH	Donald	25	Sleat INV	Inverkeithny	1	7
MACINTOSH	Edward	8	Marnoch	Marnoch	6	15
MACINTOSH	Elizabeth	4	Grange	Inverkeithny	1	11
MACINTOSH	Elizabeth	34	Forgue ABD	Inverkeithny	1	11
MACINTOSH	Elspet	4	Marnoch	Marnoch	5	5
MACINTOSH	Elspet	52	Marnoch	Marnoch	6	23
MACINTOSH	Garden	17	Marnoch	Forglen	3	1
MACINTOSH	George	2mths	Marnoch	Marnoch	5	5
MACINTOSH	George	11	Marnoch	Marnoch	6	15
MACINTOSH	George	24	Huntly ABD	Marnoch	3	15
MACINTOSH	George	19	Banff	Inverkeithny	1	6
MACINTOSH	Helen	29	Huntly ABD	Marnoch	3	2
MACINTOSH	Helen	2	Gartly ABD	Marnoch	3	2
MACINTOSH	James	10	Rothiemay	Inverkeithny	1	11
MACINTOSH	James	47	Marnoch	Marnoch	2	14
MACINTOSH	James	14	Marnoch	Marnoch	2	14
MACINTOSH	Jane	65	Marnoch	Marnoch	3	17
MACINTOSH	Jane	10	Marnoch	Marnoch	2	14
MACINTOSH	Jane	20	Marnoch	Marnoch	3	5
MACINTOSH	Janet	49	Boyndie	Marnoch	2	14
MACINTOSH	Jean	6	Marnoch	Marnoch	5	5
MACINTOSH	Jessie	7	Grange	Marnoch	3	17
MACINTOSH	John	33	Banff	Marnoch	5	4
MACINTOSH	John	22	Marnoch	Marnoch	3	2
MACINTOSH	John	28	Marnoch	Marnoch	3	17
MACINTOSH	John	50	Marnoch	Marnoch	6	15
MACINTOSH	William	21	Marnoch	Marnoch	6	15
MACINTOSH	William	14	Rothiemay	Inverkeithny	3	12
MACINTOSH	William	8	Marnoch	Marnoch	5	5
MACKAY	Alexander	45	Forgue ABD	Marnoch	6	30
MACKAY	Alexander	10	Marnoch	Marnoch	6	17
MACKAY	Ann	15 days	Marnoch	Marnoch	6	30
MACKAY	Anne	19	Marnoch	Marnoch	3	12
MACKAY	Anne	44	Rhynie ABD	Marnoch	6	30
MACKAY	Christian	35	Cairnie ABD	Marnoch	7	13
MACKAY	George	1	Marnoch	Marnoch	6	18
MACKAY	Helen	22	Marnoch	Marnoch	5	14
MACKAY	Isobel	27	Marnoch	Marnoch	1	9
MACKAY	James	24	Marnoch	Marnoch	6	8
MACKAY	Jane	79	Marnoch	Marnoch	6	25

SURNAME	CHR. NAME	AGE	BIRTH PLACE	CENSUS PARISH	BOOK	PG
MACKAY	Jane	5	Marnoch	Marnoch	6	18
MACKAY	Jane	29	Inveravon	Marnoch	3	13
MACKAY	Janet	34	Marnoch	Marnoch	6	17
MACKAY	Jean	3	Marnoch	Marnoch	1	9
MACKAY	Jean	13	Marnoch	Marnoch	5	25
MACKAY	Jessie	12	Marnoch	Marnoch	6	17
MACKAY	John	8	Marnoch	Marnoch	6	18
MACKAY	John	35	Mortlach	Marnoch	3	13
MACKAY	John	5mths	Marnoch	Marnoch	3	13
MACKAY	John	44	Garloch	Marnoch	3	12
MACKAY	John	7	Rothiemay	Marnoch	1	9
MACKAY	Joseph	3	Marnoch	Marnoch	6	18
MACKAY	Margaret	73	Marnoch	Marnoch	6	5
MACKAY	Margaret	6	Marnoch	Marnoch	6	30
MACKAY	Margaret	40	Mortlach	Marnoch	3	16
MACKAY	Mary	4	Mortlach	Marnoch	3	13
MACKAY	Mary	46	England	Marnoch	3	12
MACKAY	Mary	4	Marnoch	Marnoch	6	30
MACKAY	William	40	Marnoch	Marnoch	6	17
MACKAY	William	2	Marnoch	Marnoch	3	13
MACKAY	William	31	Marnoch	Marnoch	1	9
MACKAY	William	2 days	Marnoch	Marnoch	1	9
MACKAY	William	16	Marnoch	Marnoch	3	12
MACKENZIE	Alexander	32	Fodderty ROC	Inverkeithny	2	17
MACKENZIE	Alexander	18	Lochbroom ROC	Inverkeithny	2	2
MACKENZIE	Alexander	42	Alvah	Marnoch	5	5
MACKENZIE	Ann	37	Turriff ABD	Marnoch	5	16
MACKENZIE	Ann	26	Fetteresso KCD	Inverkeithny	2	17
MACKENZIE	Catherine	11	Marnoch	Marnoch	5	16
MACKENZIE	Donald	59	Dores INV	Inverkeithny	2	6
MACKENZIE	Eliza	9	Marnoch	Marnoch	5	16
MACKENZIE	Elspet	51	Grange	Marnoch	3	10
MACKENZIE	George	10	Forglen	Marnoch	6	5
MACKENZIE	George	20	Logie ROC	Inverkeithny	1	2
MACKENZIE	George	23	Forglen	Forglen	1	9
MACKENZIE	George	10	Forglen	Forglen	3	3
MACKENZIE	Helen	6	Forglen	Marnoch	6	5
MACKENZIE	Isabella	34	St Andrews MOR	Forglen	2	9
MACKENZIE	Isabella	3	Forglen	Marnoch	6	5
MACKENZIE	Isobel	13	Marnoch	Marnoch	5	5
MACKENZIE	Isobel	32	Alvah	Marnoch	5	23
MACKENZIE	James	38	Fyvie ABD	Forglen	2	1
MACKENZIE	James	7	Marnoch	Marnoch	5	5
MACKENZIE	James	27	Coull ABD	Inverkeithny	1	2
MACKENZIE	Jane	8	Forglen	Marnoch	6	5
MACKENZIE	Jane	29	Turriff ABD	Forglen	1	5
MACKENZIE	Janet	43	Aberlour	Marnoch	5	5
MACKENZIE	Jessie	49	Alvah	Forglen	4	2
MACKENZIE	John	27	Knockbain ROC	Inverkeithny	1	8
MACKENZIE	John	15	Marnoch	Marnoch	6	13
MACKENZIE	John	79	Auldearn NAI	Marnoch	6	13
MACKENZIE	Margaret	54	Abernethy FIF	Marnoch	6	13
MACKENZIE	Mary	8mths	Glenbervie? KCD	Inverkeithny	2	17
MACKENZIE	Mary	38	Turriff ABD	Forglen	2	1
MACKENZIE	Murdoch	20	Lochcarron ROC	Inverkeithny	2	15
MACKENZIE	Murdoch	36	Dingwall ROC	Marnoch	6	5
MACKENZIE	Sarah	55	Auchterless ABD	Marnoch	6	12
MACKENZIE	William	12	Marnoch	Marnoch	6	14
MACKENZIE	William	10	Marnoch	Marnoch	5	5
MACKENZIE	William	48	Marnoch	Marnoch	5	16
MACKENZIE	William	1	Marnoch	Marnoch	5	16
MACKENZIE	William	22	Marnoch	Marnoch	5	12
MACKIDDY	Alexander	52	Fyvie ABD	Marnoch	5	13
MACKIDDY	Ann	50	Fyvie ABD	Marnoch	5	12

SURNAME	CHR. NAME	AGE	BIRTH PLACE	CENSUS PARISH	BOOK	PG
MACKIE	Agnes	18	Forglen	Marnoch	3	4
MACKIE	Alexander	17	Forgue ABD	Marnoch	6	11
MACKIE	Ann	15	Forgue ABD	Inverkeithny	3	8
MACKIE	Henry	12	Marnoch	Marnoch	5	2
MACKIE	Isobel	49	Aberdeen ABD	Marnoch	3	4
MACKIE	James	15	Forglen	Marnoch	3	4
MACKIE	Margaret	17	Leslie ABD	Forglen	2	8
MACKIE	Peter	55	Forgue ABD	Marnoch	3	4
MACKILLIGAN	Alexander	12	Forgue ABD	Inverkeithny	1	2
MACKILLIGAN	Ann	20	Grange	Inverkeithny	1	2
MACKILLIGAN	Eliza	2	Forgue ABD	Inverkeithny	1	2
MACKILLIGAN	Isabella	26	Kinghorn FIF	Inverkeithny	1	2
MACKILLIGAN	John	13	Forgue ABD	Inverkeithny	1	2
MACKILLIGAN	John	46	Banff	Inverkeithny	1	2
MACKILLIGAN	Margaret	11	Forgue ABD	Inverkeithny	1	2
MACKILLIGAN	Mary	4	Kinghorn FIF	Inverkeithny	1	2
MACKINNON	Fanny	21	Inverkeithny	Marnoch	3	2
MACKURACH	Andrew	53	King Edward ABD	Marnoch	7	14
MACKURACH	Isabella	5	Forgue ABD	Marnoch	7	14
MACKURACH	James	20	Fordyce	Marnoch	7	14
MACKURACH	Jessie	50	Cairnie ABD	Marnoch	7	14
MACLACHLAN	Grace	32	Inveravon	Marnoch	2	6
MACLACHLAN	James	39	Inveravon	Marnoch	2	6
MACLACHLAN	Margaret	69	Kirkmichael	Marnoch	2	6
MACLACHLAN	William	39	Inveravon	Marnoch	2	6
MACLEAN	Duncan	25	Lochcarron ROC	Inverkeithny	2	15
MACLEAN	James	52	Tillacoulty CLK	Marnoch	9	5
MACLEAN	Margaret	51	Fetlar SHI	Marnoch	9	5
MACLEAN	Mary	42	Fordyce	Marnoch	6	1
MACLEAN	Sarah	13	Marnoch	Marnoch	9	5
MACLENNON	John	22	Fintray ABD	Forglen	1	5
MACLEOD	Alexander	9	Marnoch	Marnoch	6	10
MACLEOD	Barbara	7	Marnoch	Marnoch	6	10
MACLEOD	Charles S.	4	Marnoch	Marnoch	6	10
MACLEOD	Donald	32	Kincardine ROC	Marnoch	6	10
MACLEOD	Eliza	44	Keith	Marnoch	6	13
MACLEOD	Eliza	1	Marnoch	Marnoch	6	10
MACLEOD	Eliza	15	Marnoch	Marnoch	6	13
MACLEOD	Ephie	24	Loch Broom ROC	Marnoch	4	9
MACLEOD	George	1	Marnoch	Marnoch	9	5
MACLEOD	James	18	Marnoch	Marnoch	6	13
MACLEOD	James	6	Marnoch	Marnoch	6	10
MACLEOD	John	27	Kirkhill ABD	Inverkeithny	2	17
MACLEOD	John	23	Towie ABD	Inverkeithny	2	2
MACLEOD	John	53	Avoch ROC	Marnoch	6	13
MACLEOD	Kenneth	58	Strathpeffer ROC	Marnoch	8	7
MACLEOD	Malcolm	41	Inverness-shire	Marnoch	2	6
MACPHERSON	Alexander	11	Leslie ABD	Forglen	2	8
MACPHERSON	Alexander	13	Drumblade ABD	Marnoch	6	25
MACPHERSON	Alexander	58	Huntly ABD	Inverkeithny	1	5
MACPHERSON	Alexander	39	Drumnagall INV	Forglen	2	8
MACPHERSON	Ann	8	Leslie ABD	Forglen	2	8
MACPHERSON	Ann	19	Turriff ABD	Marnoch	1	1
MACPHERSON	Ann	12	Inverkeithny	Inverkeithny	1	5
MACPHERSON	Charles	19	Fordyce	Marnoch	2	9
MACPHERSON	Elizabeth	5	Drumblade ABD	Marnoch	6	26
MACPHERSON	Elizabeth	25	Inveravon	Inverkeithny	2	1
MACPHERSON	Elizabeth	4	Forglen	Forglen	2	8
MACPHERSON	Elspet	40	Leslie ABD	Forglen	2	8
MACPHERSON	Ewan	1mth	Marnoch	Marnoch	6	26
MACPHERSON	Francis	20	Inverkeithny	Inverkeithny	1	5
MACPHERSON	Helen	9	Inverkeithny	Inverkeithny	1	5
MACPHERSON	Isabel	29	Forgue ABD	Inverkeithny	1	5
MACPHERSON	JOhn	2	Forglen	Forglen	2	8

SURNAME	CHR. NAME	AGE	BIRTH PLACE	CENSUS PARISH	BOOK	PG
MACPHERSON	James	30	Boyndie	Marnoch	4	11
MACPHERSON	James	1	Marnoch	Marnoch	5	25
MACPHERSON	Janet	38	Drumblade ABD	Inverkeithny	1	5
MACPHERSON	Jean	7	Drumblade ABD	Marnoch	6	26
MACPHERSON	John	7	Inverkeithny	Inverkeithny	1	5
MACPHERSON	John	9	Drumblade ABD	Marnoch	6	25
MACPHERSON	John	42	Drumblade ABD	Marnoch	6	25
MACPHERSON	Margaret	32	Huntly ABD	Inverkeithny	1	5
MACPHERSON	Margaret	31	Drumblade ABD	Marnoch	6	25
MACPHERSON	Margaret	11	Drumblade ABD	Marnoch	6	25
MACPHERSON	Mary	6	Auchterless ABD	Forglen	2	8
MACPHERSON	Mary	23	Inverkeithny	Inverkeithny	1	5
MACPHERSON	Samuel	2	Drumblade ABD	Marnoch	6	26
MACPHERSON	William	9mths	Forglen	Forglen	2	8
MACQUEEN	Donald	68	Newhills ABD	Marnoch	3	3
MACQUEEN	Isobel	21	Newhills ABD	Marnoch	3	3
MACQUEEN	Jane	7	Inverkeithny	Inverkeithny	1	5
MACQUEEN	John	27	Newhills ABD	Marnoch	3	3
MACQUEEN	Joseph	26	Marnoch	Marnoch	6	6
MACROBERT	Alexander	31	Forglen	Forglen	3	2
MACROBERT	Alexander	64	Marnoch	Marnoch	4	17
MACROBERT	Ann	17	Forglen	Forglen	3	3
MACROBERT	Ann	23	Aberdeen ABD	Marnoch	8	1
MACROBERT	Barbara	9	Marnoch	Marnoch	4	17
MACROBERT	Barbara	21	Forglen	Forglen	3	3
MACROBERT	Barbra	16	Drumblade ABD	Marnoch	5	18
MACROBERT	Betsy	65	Marnoch	Marnoch	6	20
MACROBERT	Eliza W.	17	Marnoch	Marnoch	4	17
MACROBERT	George	21	Drumblade ABD	Marnoch	5	18
MACROBERT	George	26	Forglen	Forglen	3	3
MACROBERT	Helen	59	Forglen	Forglen	3	3
MACROBERT	Helen	50	Marnoch	Marnoch	4	17
MACROBERT	Helen	28	Forglen	Marnoch	6	5
MACROBERT	Isabella	18	Aberdeen ABD	Inverkeithny	1	6
MACROBERT	Isabella	19	Forglen	Marnoch	5	7
MACROBERT	James	57	Marnoch	Marnoch	4	17
MACROBERT	Jane	14	Drumblade ABD	Marnoch	5	19
MACROBERT	Jean	23	Forglen	Forglen	3	2
MACROBERT	Jessie	55	Dav ABD	Marnoch	5	18
MACROBERT	Jessie	10	Marnoch	Marnoch	4	17
MACROBERT	Jessie	52	King Edward ABD	Marnoch	4	17
MACROBERT	Jessie	14	Marnoch	Marnoch	4	17
MACROBERT	John	20	Forglen	Forglen	1	8
MACROBERT	John	16	Marnoch	Marnoch	4	17
MACROBERT	John	61	Forglen	Forglen	3	3
MACROBERT	Margaret	94	Turriff ABD	Forglen	3	2
MACROBERT	Peter	24	Drumblade ABD	Marnoch	5	18
MACROBERT	William	13	Drumblade ABD	Marnoch	5	19
MACROBERT	William	15	Marnoch	Marnoch	4	17
MAIN	John	22	Rathen ABD	Inverkeithny	1	2
MAIR	Margaret	57	Strichen ABD	Inverkeithny	3	4
MAIR	Margaret	12	Inverkeithny	Inverkeithny	3	4
MAIR	Morrison	21	Inverkeithny	Inverkeithny	3	2
MAIR	William	15	Inverkeithny	Inverkeithny	3	2
MALCOLM	David	17	Loggie FIF	Marnoch	6	10
MALCOLM	Elizabeth	11	Loggie FIF	Marnoch	6	10
MALCOLM	Elizabeth	52	Dunbog FIF	Marnoch	6	10
MALCOLM	Elspet	52	Marnoch	Marnoch	6	28
MALCOLM	George	26	Marnoch	Marnoch	9	7
MALCOLM	Helen	14	Loggie FIF	Marnoch	6	10
MALCOLM	Jane	23	Keith	Marnoch	9	7
MALCOLM	John	2	Keith	Marnoch	9	8
MALCOLM	Lillias	1	Keith	Marnoch	9	8
MALCOLM	Lilly	66	King Edward ABD	Marnoch	6	27

SURNAME	CHR. NAME	AGE	BIRTH PLACE	CENSUS PARISH	BOOK	PG
MALCOLM	Mary	4	Keith	Marnoch	9	8
MALCOLM	Thomas	50	Newburgh FIF	Marnoch	6	10
MANN	Barbra	6	Marnoch	Marnoch	1	7
MANN	Mary	18	Forgue ABD	Inverkeithny	2	15
MANSELL	Margraet	16	Auchterless ABD	Inverkeithny	3	6
MANSON	Charlotte D.	24	Aberdeen ABD	Inverkeithny	2	12
MARR	Barbara	9mths	Marnoch	Marnoch	8	4
MARR	Elizabeth	8	Marnoch	Marnoch	8	4
MARR	Jean	24	Huntly ABD	Marnoch	8	4
MARR	John	18	Fyvie ABD	Marnoch	8	4
MARR	Mary	2	Marnoch	Marnoch	8	4
MARR	William	37	Daviot ABD	Marnoch	8	4
MARSHALL	Alexander	9	Auchterless ABD	Inverkeithny	2	15
MARTIN	Ann	18	Marnoch	Inverkeithny	3	5
MARTIN	James	39	Longside ABD	Marnoch	3	14
MARTIN	John	11	Marnoch	Marnoch	6	13
MARTIN	Margaret	22	Fordyce	Marnoch	1	4
MARTIN	William	40	Marnoch	Marnoch	5	8
MASSIE	Catherine	36	Marnoch	Marnoch	4	10
MASSIE	Catherine	54	Marnoch	Marnoch	5	13
MASSIE	Frederick	12	Forgue ABD	Marnoch	3	15
MASSIE	Frederick	34	Forgue ABD	Marnoch	3	15
MASSIE	Joseph	65	Marnoch	Marnoch	8	7
MASSIE	Margaret	17	Marnoch	Marnoch	5	13
MASSIE	Mary	25	Marnoch	Marnoch	1	13
MATHIESON	Catherine	20	Aberdeen ABD	Forglen	1	5
MATHIESON	Jean	30	Marnoch	Marnoch	1	9
MATTHEW	Ann	50	New Deer ABD	Marnoch	6	18
MATTHEW	William	50	Methlick ABD	Marnoch	6	18
MATTHEW	William	11	Turriff ABD	Marnoch	6	18
MAVER	Elizabeth	26	Ordiquhill	Marnoch	6	12
MEARNS	Ann	5	Marnoch	Marnoch	9	3
MEARNS	Christian	30	Inverurie ABD	Marnoch	9	3
MEARNS	George	29	Leslie ABD	Marnoch	9	3
MEARNS	Georgina	1	Marnoch	Marnoch	9	3
MEARNS	Isabel	7	Marnoch	Marnoch	9	3
MEARNS	Margaret	5	Marnoch	Marnoch	9	3
MELDRUM	James	23	Marnoch	Marnoch	3	14
MELDRUM	John	14	Drumblade ABD	Forglen	4	3
MENNIE	Alexander	24	Old Rayne ABD	Forglen	2	9
MENNIE	Ann	38	Auchterless ABD	Marnoch	8	8
MENNIE	John	38	Monquhitter ABD	Forglen	2	7
MENNIE?	William	6	Marnoch	Marnoch	5	18
MERSON	Helen	18	Huntly ABD	Marnoch	1	13
MESTON	Alexander	1	Marnoch	Marnoch	4	18
MESTON	Ann	37	Peterculter ABD	Marnoch	4	18
MESTON	Archibald	36	Lumphanan ABD	Marnoch	4	18
MESTON	Archibald	3	Marnoch	Marnoch	4	18
MESTON	Charles	5	Marnoch	Marnoch	4	18
MESTON	David	9	Peterculter ABD	Marnoch	4	18
MESTON	Elizabeth	38	Lumphanan ABD	Marnoch	4	18
MESTON	Margaret	7	Marnoch	Marnoch	4	18
METHVEN	Ann	10	Marnoch	Marnoch	8	6
METHVEN	Elizabeth	18	Marnoch	Marnoch	8	6
METHVEN	Elspet	12	Marnoch	Marnoch	8	6
METHVEN	James	7	Marnoch	Marnoch	8	6
METHVEN	Janet	41	Huntly ABD	Marnoch	8	6
METHVEN	Janet	14	Marnoch	Marnoch	8	6
METHVEN	Margaret	2	Marnoch	Marnoch	8	6
METHVEN	William	50	Airlie FORFAR	Marnoch	8	6
METHVEN	William	4	Marnoch	Marnoch	8	6
MICHIE	Alexander	11	Forglen	Marnoch	8	12
MICHIE	Alexander	19	Forgue ABD	Inverkeithny	2	17
MICHIE	Ann	5	Marnoch	Marnoch	8	12

SURNAME	CHR. NAME	AGE	BIRTH PLACE	CENSUS PARISH	BOOK	PG
MICHIE	Isabella	3	Marnoch	Marnoch	8	12
MICHIE	James	14	Forglen	Marnoch	8	12
MICHIE	John	9	Forglen	Marnoch	8	12
MICHIE	Mary	7	Marnoch	Marnoch	8	12
MICHIE	Mary	42	Rothiemay	Marnoch	8	11
MICHIE	Robert	1	Marnoch	Marnoch	8	12
MICHIE	William	20	Marnoch	Marnoch	8	12
MICHIE	William	48	Drumblade ABD	Marnoch	8	11
MIDDLETON	Elizabeth	32	Turriff ABD	Inverkeithny	3	3
MIDDLETON	James	18	Inverkeithny	Inverkeithny	3	3
MIDDLETON	James	65	Ordiquhill	Inverkeithny	3	3
MIDDLETON	Janet	8	Rothiemay	Inverkeithny	3	3
MIDDLETON	Jean	25	Auchterless ABD	Inverkeithny	2	2
MIDDLETON	John	2	Inverkeithny	Inverkeithny	3	3
MIDDLETON	John	40	Rothiemay	Inverkeithny	3	3
MIDDLETON	Lily	20	Auchterless ABD	Inverkeithny	3	1
MIDDLETON	Mary	32	Inverkeithny	Inverkeithny	3	3
MILLAR	Gibson	55	Fraserburgh ABD	Inverkeithny	3	10
MILNE	Agnes	10mths	Forglen	Forglen	2	1
MILNE	Alexander	5	Marnoch	Marnoch	1	5
MILNE	Alexander	2	Marnoch	Marnoch	6	1
MILNE	Alexander	13	Grange	Marnoch	1	13
MILNE	Alexander	16	Forglen	Forglen	2	1
MILNE	Alexander	12	Marnoch	Marnoch	5	6
MILNE	Andrew	39	Botriphnie	Marnoch	1	11
MILNE	Andrew	7	Grange	Marnoch	1	11
MILNE	Ann	40	Keith	Marnoch	1	11
MILNE	Ann	47	Turriff ABD	Marnoch	5	5
MILNE	Ann	25	Turriff ABD	Marnoch	4	2
MILNE	Barbra	16	Marnoch	Marnoch	5	6
MILNE	Elizabeth	48	Turriff ABD	Inverkeithny	3	1
MILNE	Elspet	81	Forglen	Forglen	2	10
MILNE	Elspet	6	Forglen	Forglen	2	1
MILNE	Elspet	1	Rayne ABD	Forglen	2	1
MILNE	George	48	Inverkeithny	Inverkeithny	3	1
MILNE	George	10	Inverkeithny	Inverkeithny	3	1
MILNE	Helen	25	Forgue ABD	Marnoch	6	29
MILNE	Helen	10	Grange	Marnoch	1	11
MILNE	Isabella	55	Boyndie	Inverkeithny	2	1
MILNE	Isobel	39	Inverkeithny	Inverkeithny	3	1
MILNE	James	53?	Inverkeithny	Inverkeithny	2	1
MILNE	James	48	Aberdeen ABD	Marnoch	1	5
MILNE	Jane	7	Inverkeithny	Inverkeithny	3	1
MILNE	Jane	20	Cairnie ABD	Marnoch	9	8
MILNE	Janet	58	Inverkeithny	Inverkeithny	2	1
MILNE	John	51	Forglen	Forglen	2	1
MILNE	John	26	Forgue ABD	Inverkeithny	3	1
MILNE	John	1	Marnoch	Marnoch	4	2
MILNE	Margaret	16	Grange	Marnoch	1	11
MILNE	Margaret	34	Inverkeithny	Marnoch	1	5
MILNE	Margaret	22	Forglen	Forglen	2	1
MILNE	Margaret	8	Marnoch	Marnoch	5	6
MILNE	Mary	19	Marnoch	Marnoch	5	6
MILNE	Peter	3	Marnoch	Marnoch	1	11
MILNE	Robert	19	Forgue ABD	Inverkeithny	3	11
MILNE	William	20	Wick CAI	Inverkeithny	1	10
MILNE	William	3	Forglen	Forglen	2	1
MILNE	William	14	Marnoch	Marnoch	5	6
MILNE	William	54	Marnoch	Marnoch	5	5
MILNE	William	28	Forgue ABD	Marnoch	4	2
MILTON	Agnes	41	Forgue ABD	Marnoch	4	16
MILTON	Alexander	10	Marnoch	Marnoch	1	3
MILTON	Alexander	10	Marnoch	Marnoch	5	26
MILTON	Alexander	59	Rothiemay	Marnoch	1	6

SURNAME	CHR. NAME	AGE	BIRTH PLACE	CENSUS PARISH	BOOK	PG
MILTON	Alexander	4	Marnoch	Marnoch	9	1
MILTON	Ann	2	Marnoch	Marnoch	1	6
MILTON	Ann	10	Forglen	Marnoch	1	6
MILTON	Ann	51	Keith	Marnoch	1	6
MILTON	Charles	3	Marnoch	Marnoch	1	6
MILTON	Charles	9	Forglen	Marnoch	1	6
MILTON	Elizabeth	40	Gartly ABD	Marnoch	5	26
MILTON	Elspet	33	Fordyce	Marnoch	8	1
MILTON	George	17	Forglen	Marnoch	4	18
MILTON	Isobel	34	Marnoch	Marnoch	4	8
MILTON	James	26	Forglen	Marnoch	1	13
MILTON	Jean	6	Ordiquhill	Marnoch	5	26
MILTON	John	68	Rothiemay	Marnoch	1	6
MILTON	John	30	Inverkeithny	Marnoch	8	2
MILTON	Lewis	4	Marnoch	Marnoch	5	26
MILTON	Margaret	8	Ordiquhill	Marnoch	5	26
MILTON	Margaret	17	Ordiquhill	Marnoch	3	2
MILTON	William	70	Rothiemay	Marnoch	4	8
MILTON	margaret	71	Keith	Marnoch	4	8
MISSON	Charles	17	Keith	Marnoch	8	9
MITCHEL	Alexander	6	Huntly ABD	Marnoch	3	12
MITCHEL	Alexander	30	Marnoch	Marnoch	3	12
MITCHEL	Charlotte	30	Glass ABD	Marnoch	3	12
MITCHEL	Christian	8	Marnoch	Marnoch	2	11
MITCHEL	David H.	2mths	Marnoch	Marnoch	2	11
MITCHEL	Elsie	12	Marnoch	Marnoch	2	11
MITCHEL	George	1	Marnoch	Marnoch	3	13
MITCHEL	Isabella	44	Banff	Marnoch	2	11
MITCHEL	James	14	Marnoch	Marnoch	2	11
MITCHEL	Jane	20	Marnoch	Marnoch	2	11
MITCHEL	John	16	Marnoch	Marnoch	2	11
MITCHEL	John	16	Marnoch	Forglen	1	8
MITCHEL	Margaret C.	3	Marnoch	Marnoch	2	11
MITCHEL	William	6	Marnoch	Marnoch	2	11
MITCHEL	William	44	Grange	Marnoch	2	11
MITCHEL	William	3	Marnoch	Marnoch	3	12
MITCHELL	Alexander	8	Marnoch	Marnoch	1	10
MITCHELL	Ann	3	Huntly ABD	Inverkeithny	1	2
MITCHELL	Elizabeth	60	Inveravon	Marnoch	2	6
MITCHELL	Elizabeth	16	Turriff ABD	Marnoch	8	5
MITCHELL	George	3	Ordiquhill	Marnoch	2	14
MITCHELL	George	28	Marnoch	Inverkeithny	1	2
MITCHELL	George	19	Fordyce	Marnoch	4	1
MITCHELL	George	46	Macduff	Marnoch	5	9
MITCHELL	Helen	2	Marnoch	Marnoch	1	10
MITCHELL	Helen	43	Boyndie	Marnoch	1	10
MITCHELL	James	13	Rothiemay	Marnoch	1	10
MITCHELL	Jane	76	Marnoch	Forglen	4	8
MITCHELL	John	47	Ordiquhill	Marnoch	1	10
MITCHELL	Margaret	20	Boyndie	Marnoch	4	11
MITCHELL	William	24	Rothiemay	Forglen	3	1
MOFFAT	Isabella	18	Ireland	Marnoch	5	20
MOFFAT	Jane	20	Ireland	Marnoch	5	20
MOFFAT	William	31	Ireland	Marnoch	5	20
MOIR	Helen	23	Forgue ABD	Marnoch	6	2
MOIR	Isabella	34	Drumblade ABD	Inverkeithny	2	10
MOIR	Isobel	55	Marnoch	Marnoch	1	6
MOIR	James	41	Avoch ROC	Marnoch	3	12
MOIR	James	8mths	Marnoch	Marnoch	6	2
MOIR	Jane	14	Old Meldrum ABD	Marnoch	3	8
MOIR	John	23	Cairnie ABD	Marnoch	6	2
MOIR	Margaret	29	Banff	Marnoch	1	6
MOIR	Thomas	46	Knockando MOR	Inverkeithny	2	10
MOIR	William	4	Marnoch	Marnoch	6	2

SURNAME	CHR. NAME	AGE	BIRTH PLACE	CENSUS PARISH	BOOK	PG
MOIR	William	26	Forgue ABD	Marnoch	1	6
MOIR	William	52	Cairnie ABD	Marnoch	1	6
MONRO	George	16	Fordyce	Marnoch	9	2
MONTGOMERY	George	26	Fordyce	Marnoch	1	14
MORGAN	George	48	Clatt ABD	Marnoch	9	1
MORGAN	George	75	Kennethmont ABD	Marnoch	5	25
MORGAN	George	2	Marnoch	Marnoch	9	1
MORGAN	John	10mths	Marnoch	Marnoch	9	1
MORGAN	Margaret	40	Clatt ABD	Marnoch	8	7
MORGAN	Mary	28	Marnoch	Marnoch	9	1
MORISON	Alexander	50	Marnoch	Marnoch	3	14
MORISON	Ann	65	Banff	Marnoch	7	8
MORISON	Anne	28	Marnoch	Marnoch	7	14
MORISON	Christian	56	Marnoch	Marnoch	9	2
MORISON	Elizabeth	21	Marnoch	Marnoch	7	8
MORISON	Isabella	19	Marnoch	Marnoch	7	8
MORISON	James	63	Banff	Marnoch	7	9
MORISON	James	26	Marnoch	Marnoch	7	8
MORISON	Jane	23	Marnoch	Marnoch	7	8
MORISON	Jane	51	Huntly ABD	Marnoch	7	9
MORISON	Jessie	14	Marnoch	Marnoch	7	9
MORISON	John	69	Banff	Marnoch	7	8
MORISON	John	30	Marnoch	Marnoch	7	8
MORISON	Margaret	17	Marnoch	Marnoch	7	14
MORISON	William	23	Alvah	Marnoch	9	10
MORISON	William	7	Marnoch	Marnoch	7	9
MORRISON	Agnes	21	Marnoch	Marnoch	8	10
MORRISON	Alexander	4	Marnoch	Marnoch	5	16
MORRISON	Alexander	18	Rathven	Forglen	1	10
MORRISON	Alexander	2	Marnoch	Marnoch	1	6
MORRISON	Alexander	10	Marnoch	Marnoch	3	7
MORRISON	Alexander	4	Inverkeithny	Inverkeithny	3	4
MORRISON	Alexander	72	Inverkeithny	Inverkeithny	3	2
MORRISON	Alexander	1mth	Inverkeithny	Inverkeithny	2	11
MORRISON	Alexander	5	Inverkeithny	Inverkeithny	2	2
MORRISON	Alexander	45	Inverkeithny	Inverkeithny	2	1
MORRISON	Alexander	35	Marnoch	Marnoch	6	29
MORRISON	Alexander	12	Rothiemay	Marnoch	1	10
MORRISON	Alexander	2	Marnoch	Marnoch	6	29
MORRISON	Alexander	12	Marnoch	Marnoch	8	8
MORRISON	Alexander	13	Marnoch	Marnoch	8	10
MORRISON	Ann	10	Rathven	Forglen	1	10
MORRISON	Ann	45	Forgue ABD	Inverkeithny	2	1
MORRISON	Ann	69	Marnoch	Marnoch	1	1
MORRISON	Ann	59	Auchterless ABD	Marnoch	5	11
MORRISON	Ann	23	Alvah	Forglen	4	5
MORRISON	Ann	16	Inverkeithny	Inverkeithny	2	1
MORRISON	Ann	17	Ordiquhill	Marnoch	2	7
MORRISON	Ann	1	Inverkeithny	Inverkeithny	3	4
MORRISON	Barbara	77	Inverkeithny	Inverkeithny	2	1
MORRISON	Barbara	22	London	Inverkeithny	2	1
MORRISON	Barbara	55	King Edward ABD	Forglen	3	4
MORRISON	Barbara	11	Inverkeithny	Inverkeithny	2	1
MORRISON	Catherine	7mths	Marnoch	Marnoch	6	11
MORRISON	Christina	70	Forgue ABD	Marnoch	6	11
MORRISON	Christina	35	Marnoch	Marnoch	6	11
MORRISON	David	72	Banff	Forglen	1	3
MORRISON	Elizabeth	20	Rathven	Forglen	1	10
MORRISON	Elizabeth	19	Fordyce	Marnoch	5	15
MORRISON	Elizabeth	26	Forglen	Forglen	3	4
MORRISON	Elspet	60	Forglen	Marnoch	5	21
MORRISON	George	41	Fordyce	Marnoch	5	15
MORRISON	Georgina	1	Marnoch	Marnoch	2	7
MORRISON	Helen	23	Grange	Inverkeithny	3	15

SURNAME	CHR. NAME	AGE	BIRTH PLACE	CENSUS PARISH	BOOK	PG
MORRISON	Helen	17	Monquhitter ABD	Inverkeithny	3	1
MORRISON	Helen	9	Inverkeithny	Inverkeithny	2	2
MORRISON	Helen	23	Forglen	Forglen	1	7
MORRISON	Helen	10	Ordiquhill	Marnoch	2	7
MORRISON	Isabel	68	Forglen	Forglen	1	6
MORRISON	Isabel	20	Forgue ABD	Inverkeithny	2	5
MORRISON	Isabel	30	King Edward ABD	Marnoch	5	22
MORRISON	Isabel	64	Banff	Forglen	1	3
MORRISON	Isabella	15	Forglen	Forglen	3	4
MORRISON	Isabella	20	Forglen	Forglen	1	7
MORRISON	Isabella	22	Fordyce	Marnoch	8	4
MORRISON	Isabella	10	Marnoch	Marnoch	5	15
MORRISON	Isabella	48	Fordyce	Forglen	4	5
MORRISON	James	37	Tullynestle ABD	Inverkeithny	2	4
MORRISON	James	41	Marnoch	Inverkeithny	2	11
MORRISON	James	8	Inverkeithny	Inverkeithny	2	11
MORRISON	James	20	Inverkeithny	Inverkeithny	2	1
MORRISON	James	20	Forgue ABD	Inverkeithny	2	3
MORRISON	James	4	Old Machar ABD	Marnoch	6	23
MORRISON	James	11	Marnoch	Marnoch	6	29
MORRISON	James	4	Marnoch	Marnoch	1	6
MORRISON	James	4mths	Forglen	Forglen	2	6
MORRISON	James	21	Alvah	Forglen	4	5
MORRISON	James	19	Ordiquhill	Marnoch	2	7
MORRISON	James	38	Boyndie	Marnoch	2	12
MORRISON	James G.	5	Forglen	Forglen	1	10
MORRISON	Jane	7	Inverkeithny	Inverkeithny	3	4
MORRISON	Jane	14	Rathven	Forglen	1	10
MORRISON	Jane	42	Forgue ABD	Marnoch	2	7
MORRISON	Janet	34	Forgue ABD	Forglen	2	6
MORRISON	Jean	38	Forgue ABD	Inverkeithny	2	11
MORRISON	Jean	10	Marnoch	Marnoch	6	29
MORRISON	Jean	11	Marnoch	Marnoch	1	6
MORRISON	Jean	34	Forgue ABD	Marnoch	6	29
MORRISON	Jessie	8	Aberdour ABD	Marnoch	6	29
MORRISON	John	66	Inverkeithny	Inverkeithny	3	1
MORRISON	John	18	Inverkeithny	Inverkeithny	2	1
MORRISON	John	3	Forgue ABD	Inverkeithny	2	11
MORRISON	John	29	Inverkeithny	Inverkeithny	3	1
MORRISON	John	4	Marnoch	Marnoch	2	7
MORRISON	John	65	Forglen	Forglen	1	6
MORRISON	John	9	Forglen	Forglen	4	5
MORRISON	John	45	Keith	Forglen	1	10
MORRISON	John	12	Rathven	Forglen	1	10
MORRISON	John	49	Auchterless ABD	Marnoch	8	10
MORRISON	John	37	Boyndie	Marnoch	1	6
MORRISON	John	48	Fordyce	Marnoch	2	7
MORRISON	John	9	Marnoch	Marnoch	1	6
MORRISON	John	6	Marnoch	Marnoch	6	1
MORRISON	John	17	Marnoch	Marnoch	8	10
MORRISON	Margaret	27	Inverkeithny	Inverkeithny	3	1
MORRISON	Margaret	37	Rathven	Forglen	1	10
MORRISON	Margaret	6	Inverkeithny	Inverkeithny	2	11
MORRISON	Margaret	1 day	Inverkeithny	Inverkeithny	3	1
MORRISON	Margaret	60	Mortlach	Inverkeithny	3	2
MORRISON	Margaret	17	Grange	Inverkeithny	3	13
MORRISON	Margaret	7	Inverkeithny	Inverkeithny	2	2
MORRISON	Mary	48	Westruther BEW	Forglen	1	7
MORRISON	Mary	28	Drumblade ABD	Inverkeithny	2	9
MORRISON	Mary	13	Inverkeithny	Inverkeithny	2	1
MORRISON	Mary	6	Marnoch	Marnoch	1	6
MORRISON	Mary	30	King Edward ABD	Marnoch	1	6
MORRISON	Mary	9	Marnoch	Marnoch	8	10
MORRISON	Mary	7	Marnoch	Marnoch	2	7

SURNAME	CHR. NAME	AGE	BIRTH PLACE	CENSUS PARISH	BOOK	PG
MORRISON	Mary	12	Marnoch	Marnoch	5	15
MORRISON	Mary G	26	Forglen	Forglen	1	7
MORRISON	Mary G	2	Forglen	Forglen	1	10
MORRISON	Sophia	3	Inverkeithny	Inverkeithny	2	2
MORRISON	Susan	32	Marnoch	Marnoch	8	10
MORRISON	Thomas	14	Marnoch	Marnoch	4	4
MORRISON	William	19	Forglen	Forglen	1	7
MORRISON	William	20	Grange	Inverkeithny	1	2
MORRISON	William	41	Inverkeithny	Inverkeithny	3	4
MORRISON	William	30	Forglen	Marnoch	6	10
MORRISON	William	69	Mortlach	Marnoch	1	1
MORRISON	William	6	Old Machar ABD	Marnoch	6	23
MORRISON	William	29	Auchterless ABD	Forglen	2	6
MORRISON	William	8	Forglen	Forglen	1	10
MORRISON	William	12	Forglen	Forglen	4	5
MORTIMER	Alexander	47	Rayne ABD	Marnoch	1	9
MORTIMER	Benjamin	3	Marnoch	Marnoch	9	7
MORTIMER	Betty	32	Culsalmond ABD	Marnoch	9	7
MORTIMER	Eliza	6	Marnoch	Marnoch	9	7
MORTIMER	Elspet	26	Rayne ABD	Marnoch	1	1
MORTIMER	Isabel	70	Culsalmond ABD	Marnoch	9	7
MORTIMER	Jane	10mths	Marnoch	Marnoch	9	7
MORTIMER	Jean	25	Rayne ABD	Marnoch	1	9
MORTIMER	Margaret	39	Insch ABD	Marnoch	9	7
MORTIMER	William	42	Insch ABD	Marnoch	9	7
MORTIMER	William	23	Rayne ABD	Marnoch	1	9
MOWAT	Alexander	28	Waller CAI	Inverkeithny	1	8
MUNRO	Ann	13	Marnoch	Marnoch	2	5
MUNRO	Ann	44	Urray ROC	Marnoch	2	5
MUNRO	Catherine	11	Marnoch	Marnoch	2	5
MUNRO	David	45	Dundee FORFAR	Inverkeithny	3	4
MUNRO	Donald	48	Inverness INV	Marnoch	2	5
MUNRO	George	15	Huntly ABD	Marnoch	2	5
MUNRO	James	6	Marnoch	Marnoch	2	5
MUNRO	John	8	Marnoch	Marnoch	2	5
MUNROE	Christina	54	Alness ROC	Inverkeithny	2	12
MUNROE	George	1	Inverkeithny	Inverkeithny	1	4
MUNROE	Isabel	44	Drumblade ABD	Inverkeithny	1	4
MUNROE	Jane	79	Rothiemay	Inverkeithny	1	12
MUNROE	Mary	6	Inverkeithny	Inverkeithny	1	4
MUNROE	William	40	Inverkeithny	Inverkeithny	1	4
MURCHAR	Peter	45	Tarves ABD	Forglen	4	4
MURCHIE	Eliza	23	England	Marnoch	3	11
MURCHIE	George	35	Ordiquhill	Marnoch	3	11
MURCHIE	George	4	Marnoch	Marnoch	3	11
MURCHIE	John	3mths	Marnoch	Marnoch	3	11
MURCHIE	William	2	Marnoch	Marnoch	3	11
MURDO	Margaret	50	Grange	Marnoch	5	2
MURDOCH	Ann	9	Forglen	Forglen	2	2
MURDOCH	Charles	19	Turriff ABD	Inverkeithny	2	7
MURDOCH	David	27	Turriff ABD	Inverkeithny	1	3
MURDOCH	Elizabeth	11	Forglen	Forglen	3	3
MURDOCH	George	49	Fordyce	Marnoch	3	6
MURDOCH	Helen	20	Marnoch	Marnoch	6	14
MURDOCH	Henrietta	16	Ordiquhill	Marnoch	7	3
MURDOCH	Isabella	50	Fordyce	Marnoch	3	6
MURDOCH	Isobel	11	Ordiquhill	Marnoch	3	6
MURDOCH	Jemima H.G.	8	Ordiquhill	Marnoch	3	6
MURDOCH	Margaret	21	Marnoch	Inverkeithny	3	15
MURDOCH	Mary	13	Ordiquhill	Marnoch	3	6
MURDOCH	William	18	Ordiquhill	Marnoch	3	6
MURIE	Elizabeth	9	Alvah	Marnoch	7	12
MURIE	James	14	Fordyce	Marnoch	7	7
MURIE	Margaret	13	Alvah	Marnoch	7	12

SURNAME	CHR. NAME	AGE	BIRTH PLACE	CENSUS PARISH	BOOK	PG
MURIE	Robert	46	Forglen	Marnoch	8	3
MURPHY	James	7	Marnoch	Marnoch	2	1
MURRAY	Alexander	5	Marnoch	Marnoch	6	6
MURRAY	Alexander	33	Huntly ABD	Inverkeithny	1	9
MURRAY	Ann	32	Marnoch	Marnoch	6	6
MURRAY	Ann	7	Boyndie	Inverkeithny	1	9
MURRAY	Ann	67	Clatt ABD	Marnoch	5	25
MURRAY	Ann	18	Marnoch	Marnoch	1	14
MURRAY	Ann	17	Marnoch	Marnoch	5	8
MURRAY	Anne	61	Ordiquhill	Marnoch	1	11
MURRAY	Catherine	5mths	Marnoch	Marnoch	5	3
MURRAY	Catherine	35	Alvah	Marnoch	5	3
MURRAY	Charlotte	18	Drumblade ABD	Marnoch	1	14
MURRAY	David	28	Forgue ABD	Inverkeithny	2	17
MURRAY	David	3	St Nicholas ABD	Inverkeithny	2	18
MURRAY	Elizabeth	55	Turriff ABD	Marnoch	1	14
MURRAY	Elizabeth	21	Marnoch	Marnoch	8	8
MURRAY	Elspet	35	Marnoch	Inverkeithny	1	9
MURRAY	Elspet	1	Forgue ABD	Inverkeithny	1	9
MURRAY	Elspet	6	Inverkeithny	Inverkeithny	1	11
MURRAY	George	7	Marnoch	Marnoch	5	3
MURRAY	George	24	Fordyce	Marnoch	1	4
MURRAY	Helen	2	Marnoch	Marnoch	5	3
MURRAY	Isabel	27	Marnoch	Marnoch	9	8
MURRAY	James	8	Marnoch	Marnoch	5	3
MURRAY	James	50	Marnoch	Marnoch	9	2
MURRAY	James	28	Marnoch	Marnoch	1	14
MURRAY	James	21	Turriff ABD	Marnoch	1	1
MURRAY	Jane	51	Marnoch	Marnoch	2	11
MURRAY	John	65	Fordyce	Marnoch	1	14
MURRAY	John	1	St Nicholas ABD	Inverkeithny	2	18
MURRAY	John A.	10	Marnoch	Marnoch	5	3
MURRAY	Joseph	41	Marnoch	Marnoch	5	3
MURRAY	Margaret	5	Boyndie	Inverkeithny	1	9
MURRAY	Margaret	25	Macduff	Inverkeithny	2	17
MURRAY	Margaret	6	St Nicholas ABD	Inverkeithny	2	17
MURRAY	Mary	23	Marnoch	Marnoch	9	8
MURRAY	Mary	5	Marnoch	Marnoch	5	3
MURRAY	Michael	4	Marnoch	Marnoch	5	3
MURRAY	Robert	25	Boyndie	Marnoch	4	9
MURRAY	Thomas	25	Forgue ABD	Marnoch	9	3
MURRAY	William	20	Marnoch	Marnoch	8	8
MURRAY	William	5	Aberdeen ABD	Marnoch	7	9
MURRAY	William	22	Boyndie	Marnoch	9	8
MURRAY	William	82	Fordyce	Marnoch	7	9
MURRAY	William	25	Marnoch	Marnoch	3	13
MURRAY	William	16	Rothiemay	Inverkeithny	2	10
MUTCH	Elizabeth	52	Culsalmond ABD	Marnoch	6	6
MUTCH	John	14	Auchterless ABD	Inverkeithny	1	7
Martin	Mary	1	Fyvie ABD	Forglen	2	1
Michie	Jessie	5	Turriff ABD	Forglen	3	6
Michie	Jessie	5	Turriff ABD	Forglen	3	6
Middleton	Isabel	26	Aberlour	Forglen	4	3
Middleton	Isabel	26	Aberlour	Forglen	4	3
Milne	Isabella	24	Forglen	Forglen	2	1
Milne	Isabella	47	Marnoch	Forglen	2	1
Murray	Isabel	69	Rothiemay	Forglen	2	5
NAPIER	Isobel	23	Boyndie	Marnoch	2	12
NAUGHTON	Alexander	15	Forglen	Forglen	1	6
NAUGHTON	Ann	25	Banff	Forglen	1	6
NAUGHTON	Archibald	18	Forglen	Forglen	1	6
NAUGHTON	James	12	Forglen	Forglen	1	6
NAUGHTON	William	54	Monikie FORFAR	Forglen	1	6
NEACH	William	34	Fordyce	Marnoch	4	7

SURNAME	CHR. NAME	AGE	BIRTH PLACE	CENSUS PARISH	BOOK	PG
NEISH	Alexander	31	Grange	Marnoch	1	1
NEISH	Isabella	2	Marnoch	Marnoch	6	23
NEISH	James	8mths	Marnoch	Marnoch	6	23
NEISH	John	6	Grange	Marnoch	6	22
NEISH	Margaret	4mths	Grange	Marnoch	6	22
NESS	Isobel	47	Fordyce	Marnoch	2	8
NICOL	Eliza	1	Marnoch	Marnoch	6	27
NICOL	Eliza	28	Logie Buchan ABD	Marnoch	6	27
NICOL	George	38	Kennethmont ABD	Inverkeithny	1	4
NICOL	George	16	Forgue ABD	Inverkeithny	1	1
NICOL	Helen	46	Forgue ABD	Inverkeithny	1	4
NICOL	Helen	6	Inverkeithny	Inverkeithny	1	4
NICOL	James	11	Inverkeithny	Inverkeithny	1	4
NICOL	Jane	3	Marnoch	Marnoch	6	27
NICOL	John	9	Inverkeithny	Inverkeithny	1	4
NICOL	Robert	39	Fyvie ABD	Marnoch	6	27
NICOL	Robert	13	Inverkeithny	Inverkeithny	1	4
NICOL	Robert F.	4	Marnoch	Marnoch	6	27
OGG	Alexander	21	Forgue ABD	Forglen	4	6
OGG	Ann	58	Forgue ABD	Marnoch	6	11
OGG	Elizabeth	18	Forgue ABD	Marnoch	8	7
OGG	George	2	Forgue ABD	Marnoch	6	11
OGG	George	53	Forgue ABD	Forglen	4	6
OGG	George	17	Forgue ABD	Inverkeithny	2	12
OGG	Helen	19	Forgue ABD	Forglen	4	6
OGG	Janet	6	Marnoch	Marnoch	4	15
OGG	Janet	36	Fordyce	Marnoch	4	15
OGG	Jean	4	Marnoch	Marnoch	4	15
OGG	John	30	Grange	Marnoch	4	15
OGG	John	9	Forgue ABD	Forglen	4	6
OGG	Margaret	50	Forgue ABD	Forglen	4	1
OGG	Margaret	17	Forgue ABD	Forglen	4	6
OGG	Robert	18	King Edward ABD	Forglen	1	9
OGG	wife	-	-	Forglen	4	6
OGILVIE	George	50	Marnoch	Marnoch	2	5
OGSTON	Elizabeth	6	Marnoch	Marnoch	9	3
OGSTON	Helen	16	Marnoch	Marnoch	9	3
OGSTON	Isabel	46	Alvah	Marnoch	9	3
OGSTON	Isabel	2	Marnoch	Marnoch	9	3
OGSTON	James	4	Marnoch	Marnoch	9	3
OGSTON	John	58	Tyrie ABD	Marnoch	9	3
OGSTON	John	17	Alvah	Forglen	4	9
OGSTON	Rosie	22	Marnoch	Marnoch	7	12
ORD	Alexander	2	Marnoch	Marnoch	5	3
ORD	Ann	7	Rothiemay	Marnoch	5	3
ORD	Ann	11	Marnoch	Marnoch	5	9
ORD	Christian	30	Marnoch	Marnoch	5	10
ORD	Isabel	36	Cornwall ENG	Marnoch	5	3
ORD	James	47	Marnoch	Marnoch	5	9
ORD	James	71	Marnoch	Marnoch	5	2
ORD	Jane	49	Marnoch	Marnoch	5	9
ORD	Margaret	4	Rothiemay	Marnoch	5	3
ORD	William	13	Forgue ABD	Marnoch	8	12
ORD	William	37	Monquhitter ABD	Marnoch	5	10
ORD	William	1	Marnoch	Marnoch	5	10
PACKSTER	Robert	33	Rhynie ABD	Inverkeithny	2	5
PANTON	Christian	14	Marnoch	Marnoch	9	8
PARK	James	1	Inverkeithny	Inverkeithny	2	14
PARK	William	26	Udny ABD	Forglen	3	8
PATERSON	Alexander	5	Marnoch	Marnoch	7	1
PATERSON	Andrew	15	Marnoch	Forglen	1	5
PATERSON	Ann	29	Marnoch	Marnoch	7	3
PATERSON	Bathia	19	Alvah	Inverkeithny	1	8
PATERSON	Elizabeth	40	Fyvie ABD	Marnoch	7	1

SURNAME	CHR. NAME	AGE	BIRTH PLACE	CENSUS PARISH	BOOK	PG
PATERSON	Francis	6mths	Marnoch	Marnoch	7	1
PATERSON	George	10	Marnoch	Marnoch	7	1
PATERSON	Helen	13	Forglen	Forglen	4	2
PATERSON	Helen	46	Elgin MOR	Forglen	4	2
PATERSON	James	20	Fyvie ABD	Inverkeithny	2	9
PATERSON	James	42	Banff	Marnoch	7	1
PATERSON	James	11	Forglen	Forglen	4	2
PATERSON	James	17	Turriff ABD	Forglen	1	9
PATERSON	Janet	34	Marnoch	Marnoch	7	13
PATERSON	Janet	8	Forglen	Forglen	4	2
PATERSON	John	18	Marnoch	Inverkeithny	3	15
PATERSON	John	49	Resolis ROC	Forglen	4	2
PATERSON	Thomas	27	Marnoch	Marnoch	7	3
PATERSON	Thomas	51	Resolis ROC	Forglen	4	2
PATERSON	Walter	8	Marnoch	Marnoch	7	1
PATERSON	William	16	Marnoch	Marnoch	7	8
PATERSON	William	15	Turriff ABD	Forglen	1	7
PATTERSON	Alexander	8	Marnoch	Marnoch	5	16
PATTERSON	Ann	10	Marnoch	Marnoch	5	16
PATTERSON	Elizabeth	10mths	Marnoch	Marnoch	5	17
PATTERSON	George	6	Marnoch	Marnoch	5	17
PATTERSON	Henry	3	Marnoch	Marnoch	5	17
PATTERSON	William	42	Gamrie	Marnoch	5	16
PAUL	Alexander	1	Boyndie	Marnoch	2	10
PAUL	George	62	Fintray ABD	Forglen	4	1
PAUL	Isabel	23	Marnoch	Forglen	4	1
PAUL	James	2	Marnoch	Marnoch	6	13
PAUL	Jane	3	Boyndie	Marnoch	2	9
PAUL	Jessie	55	Marnoch	Forglen	4	1
PETER	Elspet	46	Alvah	Forglen	4	7
PETER	William	70	Marnoch	Forglen	4	7
PETERKIN	John	17	Gamrie	Forglen	1	9
PETERS	Barbara	74	Turriff ABD	Marnoch	8	3
PETERS	Isabella	43	Marnoch	Marnoch	8	3
PETERS	Jessie	23	Marnoch	Marnoch	3	18
PETERS	John	43	Forgue ABD	Inverkeithny	3	9
PETERS	Mary	63	Marnoch	Marnoch	3	18
PETERS	Mary	25	Marnoch	Marnoch	3	18
PETERSON	Andrew	34	Killearnan ROC	Inverkeithny	1	4
PETRIE	Ann	28	Bellie MOR	Forglen	3	1
PETRIE	Isabel Catherine	3	Drumblade ABD	Forglen	3	1
PETRIE	James	29	Dunan FORFAR	Forglen	3	1
PETRIE	Jean Thomson	5	Drumblade ABD	Forglen	3	1
PETRIE	Joseph	2	Drumblade ABD	Forglen	3	1
PETRIE	Margaret ANN	1	Huntly ABD	Forglen	3	1
PHILIP	George	41	Glass ABD	Marnoch	5	15
PHILIPS	James	24	England	Forglen	1	9
PIRIE	Alexander	22	Marnoch	Marnoch	2	6
PIRIE	Ann	22	Marnoch	Marnoch	5	7
PIRIE	Barbara	17	King Edward ABD	Forglen	2	9
PIRIE	Christian	16	Marnoch	Marnoch	9	4
PIRIE	Elizabeth	19	Grange	Marnoch	9	10
PIRIE	Elizabeth	35	Turriff ABD	Marnoch	7	12
PIRIE	George	39	Banff	Marnoch	7	12
PIRIE	George	55	Turriff ABD	Inverkeithny	3	11
PIRIE	George	15	Inverkeithny	Inverkeithny	3	11
PIRIE	Helen	21	Marnoch	Marnoch	9	9
PIRIE	Isabella	18	Turriff ABD	Marnoch	8	7
PIRIE	Isabella	30	Glass ABD	Marnoch	3	15
PIRIE	James	16	Marnoch	Marnoch	2	10
PIRIE	James	3mths	Marnoch	Marnoch	7	12
PIRIE	James	40	Inverkeithny	Marnoch	2	10
PIRIE	Janet	57	Rothiemay	Inverkeithny	3	11
PIRIE	Janet	40	Marnoch	Marnoch	2	10

SURNAME	CHR. NAME	AGE	BIRTH PLACE	CENSUS PARISH	BOOK	PG
PIRIE	Jessie	18	Inverkeithny	Inverkeithny	3	11
PIRIE	John	38	Inverkeithny	Inverkeithny	1	7
PIRIE	John	4	Marnoch	Marnoch	7	12
PIRIE	Margaret	1	King Edward ABD	Marnoch	7	12
PIRIE	Margaret	19	Alvah	Forglen	4	1
PIRIE	Mary	6	Banff	Marnoch	7	12
PIRIE	Mary	17	Auchterless ABD	Inverkeithny	1	7
PIRIE	Mary A.	9	Marnoch	Marnoch	6	17
PIRIE	Robert	6	Marnoch	Marnoch	6	14
PIRIE	William	30	Glass ABD	Marnoch	3	15
PIRIE	William	4	Marnoch	Marnoch	5	20
PIRIE	William	2	Marnoch	Marnoch	7	12
PIRRIE	Ann	9	Marnoch	Marnoch	1	7
PIRRIE	Charles	2	Marnoch	Marnoch	1	8
PIRRIE	John	7	Marnoch	Marnoch	1	8
PIRRIE	Margaret	42	Marnoch	Marnoch	1	7
PIRRIE	Margaret	15	Ordiquhill	Marnoch	1	7
PIRRIE	Sophia	11	Marnoch	Marnoch	1	7
PIRRIE	William	41	Keith	Marnoch	1	7
PIRRIE	William	5	Marnoch	Marnoch	1	8
PORTER	Barbara	84	Marnoch	Marnoch	6	28
PORTER	George	8	Marnoch	Marnoch	6	28
PORTER	Jane	72	Marnoch	Marnoch	9	5
PORTER	Mary	46	Turriff ABD	Marnoch	5	5
PORTERFIELD	(male)	1mth	Marnoch	Marnoch	1	12
PORTERFIELD	Alexander	9	Inverkeithny	Marnoch	1	12
PORTERFIELD	Ann	11	Inverkeithny	Marnoch	1	12
PORTERFIELD	Christian	3	Inverkeithny	Marnoch	1	12
PORTERFIELD	Helen	6	Inverkeithny	Marnoch	1	12
PORTERFIELD	Helen	43	Auchterless ABD	Marnoch	1	11
PORTERFIELD	Isabella	38	Keith	Forglen	2	5
PORTERFIELD	Margaret	15	Forgue ABD	Marnoch	1	11
PORTERFIELD	Peter	16	Forgue ABD	Marnoch	1	11
PORTERFIELD	Peter	40	Grange	Marnoch	1	11
PORTERFIELD	William	25	Grange	Marnoch	1	12
PORTERFIELD	William	13	Inverkeithny	Marnoch	1	11
PORTIS	George	29	Grange	Marnoch	5	23
PORTIS	George	2	Marnoch	Marnoch	5	23
PORTIS	Margaret	3	Marnoch	Marnoch	5	23
PORTIS	Margaret	27	Marnoch	Marnoch	5	23
PRICE	Christian	84	Marnoch	Marnoch	9	9
PRICE	Elizabeth	49	Marnoch	Marnoch	9	9
PRICE	Jane	56	Marnoch	Marnoch	9	9
PRICE	William	45	Marnoch	Marnoch	9	9
PROCTOR	Margaret	22	Forglen	Marnoch	8	2
RAE	Alexander	65	Forglen	Marnoch	9	4
RAE	Ann	22	Forglen	Marnoch	9	4
RAE	Christian	65	Cairnie ABD	Marnoch	1	8
RAE	David	17	Forglen	Forglen	1	2
RAE	Elizabeth	50	Forglen	Forglen	1	2
RAE	Elspet	55	Forglen	Forglen	4	8
RAE	Elspet	55	Banff	Marnoch	9	4
RAE	Elspet	21	Fordyce	Marnoch	4	1
RAE	Isabella	20	Forglen	Forglen	1	2
RAE	James	20	Marnoch	Marnoch	9	4
RAE	Jane	24	Forglen	Marnoch	9	4
RAE	John	18	Forglen	Forglen	3	2
RAE	John	80	Forglen	Forglen	1	2
RAE	John	15	Marnoch	Marnoch	4	10
RAE	Joseph	15	Forglen	Forglen	1	4
RAE	Margaret	28	Forglen	Forglen	4	8
RAE	William	14	Alvah	Forglen	2	7
RAE	William	55	Forglen	Forglen	4	8
RAEBURN	Adam	40	Banff	Marnoch	2	1

SURNAME	CHR. NAME	AGE	BIRTH PLACE	CENSUS PARISH	BOOK	PG
RAEBURN	Alexander	31	Banff	Marnoch	2	2
RAEBURN	Alexander	30	Forgue ABD	Inverkeithny	1	7
RAEBURN	Barbara	25	Insch ABD	Inverkeithny	1	12
RAEBURN	Barbara	3	Marnoch	Marnoch	3	4
RAEBURN	Barbara	33	Banff	Marnoch	2	1
RAEBURN	Jane	11	Turriff ABD	Marnoch	3	4
RAEBURN	Jane	22	Forgue ABD	Marnoch	7	9
RAEBURN	Jessie	9mths	Marnoch	Marnoch	3	4
RAEBURN	Jessie	31	Turriff ABD	Marnoch	3	4
RAEBURN	John	9	Marnoch	Marnoch	3	4
RAEBURN	Margaret	16	Forgue ABD	Inverkeithny	1	7
RAEBURN	Margaret	70	Keith	Marnoch	2	1
RAEBURN	Margaret	7	Marnoch	Marnoch	3	4
RAEBURN	Robert	28	Ordiquhill	Inverkeithny	1	12
RAEBURN	William	31	Banff	Marnoch	3	4
RAINY	Charles	21	Upper Banchory KCD	Marnoch	2	5
RAINY	George	14	Marnoch	Marnoch	3	8
RAINY	James	22	Marnoch	Marnoch	3	14
RAINY	Jane	27	Fordyce	Marnoch	5	11
RANIE	Christian	47	Chapel of Garioch ABD	Marnoch	6	22
RANIE	George	9	Marnoch	Marnoch	6	22
RANIE	James	41	Aberlour	Marnoch	6	22
RANIE	Jane	2	Marnoch	Marnoch	6	23
RANKEN	Ann	3	Gartly ABD	Marnoch	7	4
RANKEN	Brice	56	Aberdeen ABD	Marnoch	7	4
RANKEN	Brice	32	Rothiemay	Marnoch	7	4
RANKEN	Caroline	16	Cairnie ABD	Marnoch	7	4
RANKEN	Helen	57	Cairnie ABD	Marnoch	7	4
RANNIE	Alexander	19	Fyvie ABD	Marnoch	5	14
RANNIE	Andrew	9mths	Alvah	Marnoch	5	5
RANNIE	Ann	24	Marnoch	Forglen	2	4
RANNIE	Ann	13	Marnoch	Marnoch	5	13
RANNIE	Catherine	45	Glass ABD	Marnoch	6	9
RANNIE	Elizabeth	53	Fyvie ABD	Marnoch	5	14
RANNIE	Elspet	21	Fyvie ABD	Forglen	1	1
RANNIE	George	50	Marnoch	Marnoch	5	5
RANNIE	James	7	Marnoch	Marnoch	6	9
RANNIE	Janet	84	Marnoch	Marnoch	1	6
RANNIE	Janet	76	Forglen	Forglen	2	4
RANNIE	Jean	86	Marnoch	Marnoch	1	6
RANNIE	John	48	Marnoch	Marnoch	6	9
RANNIE	John	10	Marnoch	Marnoch	6	9
RANNIE	John	12	Chapel of Garioch ABD	Marnoch	1	14
RANNIE	Margaret	2	Marnoch	Marnoch	6	9
RANNIE	Margaret	18	Fyvie ABD	Marnoch	5	14
RANNIE	Mary	18	Marnoch	Marnoch	5	5
RANNIE	Robert	17	Marnoch	Marnoch	6	9
RATTERAY	James	19	Inveravon	Marnoch	2	4
RATTERAY	John	41	Inveravon	Marnoch	2	4
REARY	James	19	Inverkeithny	Marnoch	7	3
REDFORD	Alexander	14	Marnoch	Marnoch	7	5
REDFORD	Alexander	18	Marnoch	Marnoch	9	6
REDFORD	Christian	17	Marnoch	Marnoch	9	2
REDFORD	Elizabeth	72	Marnoch	Marnoch	8	1
REDFORD	Elspet	10	Marnoch	Marnoch	9	2
REDFORD	Elspet	50	Marnoch	Marnoch	9	2
REDFORD	George	5	Marnoch	Marnoch	6	16
REDFORD	James	38	Marnoch	Marnoch	3	8
REDFORD	James	42	Marnoch	Marnoch	9	2
REDFORD	James	43	Marnoch	Marnoch	9	2
REDFORD	James	21	Marnoch	Marnoch	9	2
REDFORD	Janet	20	Marnoch	Marnoch	6	11
REDFORD	John	9	Marnoch	Cernsoch	9	2
REDFORD	Margaret	29	Marnoch	Marnoch	3	1

SURNAME	CHR. NAME	AGE	BIRTH PLACE	CENSUS PARISH	BOOK	PG
REDFORD	Margaret	69	Marnoch	Marnoch	9	2
REDFORD	Margaret	12	Marnoch	Marnoch	9	2
REDFORD	Thomas	8	Marnoch	Marnoch	9	2
REDFORD	William	14	Marnoch	Marnoch	9	2
REID	Alexander	73	Boyndie	Marnoch	4	18
REID	Alexander	12	Fordyce	Marnoch	3	14
REID	Alexander	4	Marnoch	Marnoch	5	2
REID	Alexander	11	Forgue ABD	Inverkeithny	2	12
REID	Andrew	30	Auchterless ABD	Forglen	1	5
REID	Ann	45	Marnoch	Marnoch	6	28
REID	Ann	19	Aberdeenshire	Inverkeithny	2	12
REID	Ann	20	Ordiquhill	Marnoch	5	20
REID	Ann	79	Marnoch	Marnoch	5	15
REID	Catherine	50	Gamrie	Forglen	3	6
REID	Catherine	12	Marnoch	Marnoch	4	18
REID	Charles	24	Marnoch	Marnoch	4	18
REID	Christian	69	Boyndie	Marnoch	3	10
REID	Christian	56	Marnoch	Marnoch	9	6
REID	Christian	68	Insch ABD	Marnoch	4	13
REID	Edward M.	7	Turriff ABD	Marnoch	3	14
REID	Elspet	25	Auchindoir ABD	Marnoch	6	22
REID	George	1	Alvah	Marnoch	6	24
REID	George	3	Marnoch	Marnoch	5	11
REID	George	15	Kennethmont ABD	Marnoch	3	13
REID	Helen	8	Marnoch	Marnoch	5	2
REID	Helen	31	Forgue ABD	Marnoch	1	13
REID	Helen	41	Marnoch	Marnoch	5	2
REID	Isabella	26	Turriff ABD	Forglen	3	6
REID	Isabella	42	Forgue ABD	Inverkeithny	1	11
REID	James	52	Marnoch	Marnoch	1	13
REID	James	10mths	Marnoch	Marnoch	1	13
REID	James	10	Marnoch	Marnoch	9	6
REID	James	48	Forfarshire	Inverkeithny	1	11
REID	James	6	Marnoch	Marnoch	1	5
REID	Jane	40	Grange	Marnoch	5	11
REID	Jane	10	Raffan BAN	Marnoch	5	11
REID	Janet	83	Fordyce	Marnoch	5	20
REID	Janet	22	Ordiquhill	Marnoch	5	20
REID	Jean	53	Cairnie ABD	Marnoch	4	14
REID	John	42	Alvah	Marnoch	3	14
REID	Margaret	13	Auchterless? ABD	Inverkeithny	2	18
REID	Margaret	48	Forgue ABD	Inverkeithny	2	12
REID	Margaret	4	Marnoch	Marnoch	3	14
REID	Margaret	11	Turriff ABD	Forglen	3	6
REID	Mary	9	Turriff ABD	Marnoch	3	14
REID	Mary	16	Forgue ABD	Inverkeithny	2	12
REID	Mary	10	Marnoch	Marnoch	5	2
REID	Mary	67	Marnoch	Marnoch	4	18
REID	Mary	43	Fordyce	Marnoch	3	14
REID	Peter	58	Insch ABD	Marnoch	4	13
REID	Peter	58	Marnoch	Marnoch	6	28
REID	Robert	18	Forgue ABD	Inverkeithny	2	8
REID	Robert	16	Turriff ABD	Forglen	3	6
REID	Robert	52	New Deer ABD	Forglen	3	6
REID	Thomas	9	Rothiemay	Inverkeithny	1	11
REID	William	16	Fordyce	Marnoch	3	14
REID	William	1	Marnoch	Marnoch	5	11
REID	William	20	Turriff ABD	Marnoch	1	14
REID	William	47	Turriff ABD	Marnoch	9	6
REID	William	22	Marnoch	Forglen	1	1
REID	William	27	Marnoch	Marnoch	4	14
REID	William	12	Rothiemay	Inverkeithny	1	11
REID?	James	2	Turriff ABD	Forglen	3	6
REIDFORD	Christina	2	Marnoch	Marnoch	4	1

SURNAME	CHR. NAME	AGE	BIRTH PLACE	CENSUS PARISH	BOOK	PG
REIDFORD	Elizabeth	2	Marnoch	Marnoch	4	1
REIDFORD	George	36	Marnoch	Marnoch	4	1
REIDFORD	George	8	Marnoch	Marnoch	4	1
REIDFORD	Isabella	12	Marnoch	Marnoch	4	1
REIDFORD	Isabella	37	Forglen	Marnoch	4	1
REIDFORD	James	72	Marnorch	Inverkeithny	3	15
REIDFORD	John	6	Marnoch	Marnoch	4	1
REIDFORD	Robert	10	Marnoch	Marnoch	4	1
REIDHRI	Mary	46	Rayne ABD	Inverkeithny	3	11
RENNER	William	12	Inverkeithny	Inverkeithny	3	11
RENNIE	George	27	Banff	Inverkeithny	2	8
REPAR	George	9mths	Forglen	Forglen	3	9
RIACH	Eliza	54	Aberdeen ABD	Marnoch	6	27
RIACH	Mary	58	Boyndie	Marnoch	3	8
RICHARDSON	Mary	67	Cairnie ABD	Marnoch	5	19
RIDDOCH	Alexander	22	Alvah	Marnoch	4	6
RIDDOCH	Isabella	45	Fordyce	Forglen	3	5
RIDDOCH	John	20	Rothiemay	Forglen	2	9
RIDDOCH	John	3	Marnoch	Marnoch	5	3
RIDDOCH	male	1mth	Marnoch	Marnoch	3	2
RITCHIE	Ann	71	Forglen	Marnoch	7	2
RITCHIE	Elizabeth	40	Marnoch	Marnoch	6	25
RITCHIE	Helen	30	Alvah	Marnoch	7	2
RITCHIE	James	43	Marnoch	Marnoch	6	24
RITCHIE	John	30	Marnoch	Marnoch	7	2
RITCHIE	William	5	Marnoch	Marnoch	6	25
ROBB	Ann	1	Forglen	Forglen	1	9
ROBB	Ann	25	Forglen	Forglen	1	9
ROBB	George	34	Tarves ABD	Forglen	1	9
ROBB	George	6	Forglen	Forglen	1	9
ROBB	George	5	Forgue ABD	Marnoch	6	14
ROBB	James	2	Forglen	Forglen	1	9
ROBB	James Fraser	23	Huntly ABD	Marnoch	2	2
ROBB	John	3	Forglen	Forglen	1	7
ROBB	Mary	62	Clatt ABD	Marnoch	6	12
ROBB	Mary	5	Forglen	Forglen	1	9
ROBERTSON	Alexander	28	Portsoy	Marnoch	6	30
ROBERTSON	Alexander	2	Boyndie	Marnoch	5	26
ROBERTSON	Alexander	35	Marnoch	Marnoch	3	8
ROBERTSON	Alexander G.	2	Marnoch	Marnoch	8	2
ROBERTSON	Ann	37	Cairnie ABD	Marnoch	8	12
ROBERTSON	Ann	17	Marnoch	Marnoch	1	12
ROBERTSON	Ann	29	Rothiemay	Marnoch	2	2
ROBERTSON	Anne	28	Rathven	Marnoch	6	30
ROBERTSON	Barbara	4	Methlick ABD	Forglen	3	6
ROBERTSON	Catherine	8mths	Marnoch	Marnoch	8	2
ROBERTSON	Elizabeth	30	Boyndie	Marnoch	5	26
ROBERTSON	Elizabeth	58	Marnoch	Forglen	1	3
ROBERTSON	Elspet	10	Marnoch	Marnoch	8	2
ROBERTSON	Elspet	6	Marnoch	Marnoch	6	3
ROBERTSON	Elspet	42	Fyvie ABD	Marnoch	8	2
ROBERTSON	Elspet	69	Marnoch	Inverkeithny	1	11
ROBERTSON	Francis	12	Forglen	Forglen	4	2
ROBERTSON	George	79	Marnoch	Marnoch	6	7
ROBERTSON	George	32	Cairnie ABD	Marnoch	3	13
ROBERTSON	George	28	Alvah	Inverkeithny	3	1
ROBERTSON	Helen	5	Marnoch	Marnoch	8	4
ROBERTSON	Helen	17	Forglen	Forglen	4	2
ROBERTSON	Isabel	21	Marnoch	Marnoch	9	7
ROBERTSON	Isabella	8	Marnoch	Marnoch	8	2
ROBERTSON	Isabella	24	Keith	Marnoch	3	15
ROBERTSON	Isabella	61	Forgue ABD	Marnoch	5	14
ROBERTSON	Isabella	3mths	Boyndie	Marnoch	5	26
ROBERTSON	Isobel	50	Ordiquhill	Marnoch	1	12

SURNAME	CHR. NAME	AGE	BIRTH PLACE	CENSUS PARISH	BOOK	PG
ROBERTSON	James	43	Culsalmond ABD	Marnoch	8	2
ROBERTSON	James	4	Marnoch	Marnoch	8	2
ROBERTSON	James	6	Marnoch	Marnoch	5	21
ROBERTSON	James	1	Marnoch	Marnoch	3	8
ROBERTSON	James	37	Marnoch	Inverkeithny	1	6
ROBERTSON	James	25	Ordiquhill	Forglen	2	2
ROBERTSON	James	73	Marnoch	Marnoch	5	14
ROBERTSON	Jane	23	Forgue ABD	Inverkeithny	1	6
ROBERTSON	Jane	1	Inverkeithny	Inverkeithny	1	6
ROBERTSON	Jane	2	Rothiemay	Marnoch	2	2
ROBERTSON	Jane	32	Rothiemay	Marnoch	3	8
ROBERTSON	Jean	16	Monquhitter ABD	Inverkeithny	3	8
ROBERTSON	Jean	32	Methlick ABD	Forglen	3	6
ROBERTSON	Jean	50	Forglen	Marnoch	1	12
ROBERTSON	John	3	Marnoch	Marnoch	6	30
ROBERTSON	Margaret	48	Marnoch	Marnoch	2	10
ROBERTSON	Margaret	68	Rothiemay	Marnoch	1	8
ROBERTSON	Margaret	13	Marnoch	Marnoch	1	12
ROBERTSON	Mary	50	Forglen	Forglen	4	2
ROBERTSON	Mary	69	Auldearn NAI	Marnoch	6	7
ROBERTSON	Mary	26	Forgue ABD	Inverkeithny	1	11
ROBERTSON	Mary	82	Grange	Marnoch	1	12
ROBERTSON	Mary	38	Marnoch	Marnoch	2	13
ROBERTSON	Mary	29	Marnoch	Marnoch	5	14
ROBERTSON	Mary	1	Marnoch	Marnoch	6	30
ROBERTSON	Mary	14	Monquhitter ABD	Marnoch	8	2
ROBERTSON	Theodore	4	Rothiemay	Marnoch	2	2
ROBERTSON	Thomas	64?	Gartly ABD	Inverkeithny	1	11
ROBERTSON	William	4	Boyndie	Marnoch	5	26
ROBERTSON	William	54	New Deer ABD	Marnoch	1	12
ROBERTSON	William	31	Huntly ABD	Marnoch	2	2
ROBERTSON	William	13	Alvah	Marnoch	9	6
ROBERTSON	William	56	Huntly ABD	Forglen	1	3
ROBERTSON	William	80	Marnoch	Marnoch	1	12
ROBERTSON	isabella	80	Ordiquhill	Marnoch	2	10
ROBSON	Alexander	78	Banff	Marnoch	8	4
ROBSON	David	1	Marnoch	Marnoch	5	22
ROBSON	James	38	Marnoch	Marnoch	5	22
ROBSON	James	3	Marnoch	Marnoch	4	1
ROBSON	Jean	71	Marnoch	Marnoch	8	4
ROBSON	Sarah	33	Marnoch	Marnoch	5	22
ROBSON	William	5	London ENG	Marnoch	5	22
ROLLO	Janet Graham	27	Edinburgh MLN	Forglen	2	9
RONALD	Christian	55	Marnoch	Marnoch	9	9
ROSE	Mary	20	Gartly ABD	Marnoch	3	17
ROSS	Alexander	24	Fordyce	Marnoch	8	5
ROSS	Alexander	4	Inverkeithny	Marnoch	3	4
ROSS	Alexander	16	Marnoch	Marnoch	1	1
ROSS	Ann	5	Gartly ABD	Forglen	4	9
ROSS	Donald	16	Skene ABD	Inverkeithny	2	13
ROSS	Elizabeth	40	Forglen	Marnoch	5	21
ROSS	Elspet	11mths	Marnoch	Marnoch	3	4
ROSS	Henry	20	Coull ABD	Forglen	1	5
ROSS	Isabel	28	Marnoch	Marnoch	5	18
ROSS	James	26	Fordyce	Marnoch	3	3
ROSS	James	2	Inverkeithny	Marnoch	3	4
ROSS	Jane	29	Inverkeithny	Marnoch	3	3
ROSS	Janet	60	Marnoch	Marnoch	5	17
ROSS	Jean	13	Rothiemay	Marnoch	5	15
ROSS	Jessie	25	Marnoch	Marnoch	5	17
ROSS	Margaret	6	Marnoch	Marnoch	7	5
ROSS	Roderick	18	Inverness INV	Forglen	3	8
ROSS	Roderick	27	Clyne SUT	Forglen	2	1
ROSS	William	27	Huntly ABD	Inverkeithny	2	1

SURNAME	CHR. NAME	AGE	BIRTH PLACE	CENSUS PARISH	BOOK	PG
ROSS	William	23	Marnoch	Marnoch	5	18
ROSS	William	23	Kincardine ROC	Marnoch	2	8
ROY	Bell	42	Marnoch	Marnoch	7	10
ROY	George	39	Marnoch	Marnoch	7	10
ROY	Jane	16	Marnoch	Marnoch	1	14
ROY	John	19	Alvah	Marnoch	7	10
RUDDACH	Isobel	86	Marnoch	Marnoch	6	11
RUDDIMAN	Barbra	20	Marnoch	Marnoch	5	13
RUDDIMAN	Elizabeth	7	Turriff ABD	Marnoch	5	14
RUDDIMAN	James	58	Alvah	Marnoch	5	13
RUDDIMAN	Jane	52	Marnoch	Marnoch	5	13
RUDDIMAN	Mary	14	Marnoch	Marnoch	5	13
RUDIMAN	Ann	25	Marnoch	Marnoch	1	10
RUSSEL	Alexander	25	Forgue ABD	Marnoch	9	6
RUSSEL	Alexander	2	Marnoch	Marnoch	2	11
RUSSEL	Alexander	58	Rothes MOR	Marnoch	5	18
RUSSEL	Alexander	3	Marnoch	Marnoch	9	6
RUSSEL	Christian	21	Marnoch	Marnoch	5	18
RUSSEL	David	20	Duffus MOR	Inverkeithny	1	10
RUSSEL	Elizabeth	27	Forgue ABD	Marnoch	1	4
RUSSEL	George	22	Forgue ABD	Marnoch	9	6
RUSSEL	George	22	Marnoch	Marnoch	5	18
RUSSEL	Helen	31	Marnoch	Marnoch	9	6
RUSSEL	Isabella	24	Forgue ABD	Marnoch	2	11
RUSSEL	James	5	Marnoch	Marnoch	9	6
RUSSEL	James	1	Marnoch	Marnoch	2	11
RUSSEL	James	9	Marnoch	Marnoch	1	4
RUSSEL	James	58	Fordyce	Marnoch	1	4
RUSSEL	James	34	Deskford	Marnoch	2	11
RUSSEL	Lillias	2	Marnoch	Marnoch	9	6
RUSSEL	Mary	4	Forgue ABD	Marnoch	2	11
RUSSELL	Jean	48	Keith	Marnoch	5	2
RUXTON	James	6	Old Deer ABD	Marnoch	6	27
SANDIESON	Agnes	93	Inverkeithny	Inverkeithny	2	18
SANDIESON	Alexander	24	Inverkeithny	Inverkeithny	2	18
SANDIESON	George	7mths	Auchterless? ABD	Inverkeithny	2	18
SANDIESON	James	64	Inverkeithny	Inverkeithny	2	18
SANDIESON	Margaret	62	Keith	Inverkeithny	2	18
SANDISON	Elspet	35	Auchterless ABD	Inverkeithny	3	10
SANDISON	George	64	Rothiemay	Marnoch	1	10
SANDISON	George	57	Ordiquhill	Inverkeithny	3	10
SANDISON	Jean	33	Huntly ABD	Marnoch	1	10
SANGSTER	John	17	Monquhitter ABD	Inverkeithny	3	6
SCOTT	Charles	22	Boyndie	Marnoch	8	8
SCOTT	James	9	Huntly ABD	Marnoch	2	4
SCOTT	John	37	Forgue ABD	Inverkeithny	3	12
SCOTT	John	22	Fyvie ABD	Marnoch	8	8
SCOTT	Rachel	34	Kineff KCD	Forglen	1	5
SHAND	Alexander	3	Marnoch	Marnoch	3	8
SHAND	Ann	18	Insch ABD	Forglen	4	4
SHAND	Ann	27	Marnoch	Forglen	2	5
SHAND	Ann	22	Forgue ABD	Inverkeithny	2	8
SHAND	Ann	67	Marnoch	Marnoch	5	21
SHAND	Bell	24	Marnoch	Marnoch	7	2
SHAND	Catherine	2	Forglen	Marnoch	5	18
SHAND	Christian	23	Forglen	Marnoch	4	3
SHAND	Eliza	20	Forgue ABD	Inverkeithny	2	10
SHAND	Elspet	3	Forgue ABD	Inverkeithny	2	14
SHAND	George	5	Forgue ABD	Inverkeithny	2	14
SHAND	Helen	11mths	Marnoch	Marnoch	7	2
SHAND	James	53	Marnoch	Marnoch	6	1
SHAND	Jane	52	Forgue ABD	Marnoch	7	2
SHAND	Jane	22	Marnoch	Marnoch	1	13
SHAND	Jane	3	Marnoch	Marnoch	7	2

SURNAME	CHR. NAME	AGE	BIRTH PLACE	CENSUS PARISH	BOOK	PG
SHAND	Jane	33	Rothes MOR	Marnoch	3	8
SHAND	Janet	1	Inverkeithny	Inverkeithny	2	14
SHAND	Janet	28	Marnoch	Marnoch	6	1
SHAND	Jean	24	Marnoch	Marnoch	6	1
SHAND	Jean	45	Prenmay ABD	Inverkeithny	2	14
SHAND	Jean	11	Insch ABD	Inverkeithny	2	14
SHAND	Jean	27	Forgue ABD	Inverkeithny	2	7
SHAND	John	67	Keith	Inverkeithny	2	1
SHAND	John	15	Marnoch	Marnoch	7	2
SHAND	John	1	Marnoch	Marnoch	3	8
SHAND	Margaret	27	Forgue ABD	Marnoch	5	27
SHAND	Margaret	8	Forgue ABD	Inverkeithny	2	14
SHAND	Margaret	3mths	Marnoch	Marnoch	6	12
SHAND	Peter	35	Mortlach	Marnoch	3	8
SHAND	Robert	46	Cabrach	Inverkeithny	2	14
SHAND	William	44	Forgue ABD	Marnoch	7	2
SHAND	William	24	Marnoch	Marnoch	3	14
SHARP	Adam	15	Forgue ABD	Inverkeithny	3	6
SHARP	James	74	Marnoch	Marnoch	5	2
SHARP	James	20	Forgue ABD	Inverkeithny	2	13
SHEARER	Ann	37	Turriff ABD	Inverkeithny	2	7
SHEARER	Charles	15	Ordiquhill	Marnoch	4	3
SHEARER	Christian	28	Aberdeen ABD	Forglen	2	10
SHEARER	Elizabeth	26	Cairnie ABD	Marnoch	3	12
SHEARER	Geo	2	Strichen ABD	Forglen	2	10
SHEARER	Isabel	74	Inverkeithny	Forglen	2	10
SHEARER	Isobel	54	Mortlach	Marnoch	3	12
SHEARER	James	32	Marnoch	Forglen	2	10
SHEARER	James	44	Marnoch	Marnoch	3	7
SHEARER	Jean	8	Auchterless ABD	Inverkeithny	2	7
SHEARER	John	59	Cairnie ABD	Marnoch	3	12
SHEARER	John	18	Turriff ABD	Inverkeithny	2	7
SHEARER	William	47	Turriff ABD	Inverkeithny	2	7
SHEPHERD	Alexander	37	Forgue ABD	Marnoch	4	10
SHERAR	William	12	Turriff ABD	Marnoch	9	2
SHERIFFS	Anne	28	Forglen	Marnoch	3	6
SHERIFFS	Hugh	16	Marnoch	Marnoch	7	13
SHERIFFS	Isabella	15	Marnoch	Marnoch	7	13
SHERIFFS	James	1	Marnoch	Marnoch	3	6
SHERIFFS	James	54	Ordiquhill	Marnoch	7	13
SHERIFFS	William	4	Marnoch	Marnoch	7	13
SHIRER	Elspet	69	Marnoch	Marnoch	7	9
SHIRER	William	29	Marnoch	Marnoch	7	10
SIEVEWRIGHT	Helen	13	Marnoch	Marnoch	4	3
SIEVEWRIGHT	James	80	Boyndie	Marnoch	5	14
SIEVEWRIGHT	Jane	11	Marnoch	Marnoch	2	11
SIEVEWRIGHT	Mary	3	Marnoch	Marnoch	5	14
SIM	Alexander	7	Marnoch	Marnoch	5	10
SIM	Alexander	4	Marnoch	Marnoch	8	3
SIM	Alexander	23	Rathven	Forglen	2	10
SIM	Ann	10	Marnoch	Marnoch	5	10
SIM	Ann	21	Marnoch	Marnoch	7	10
SIM	Ann	33	Marnoch	Marnoch	8	3
SIM	Barbara	59	Culsalmond ABD	Marnoch	3	17
SIM	Christian	17	Fyvie ABD	Marnoch	2	12
SIM	Elisa	16	Huntly ABD	Forglen	3	1
SIM	Elizabeth	15	Mortlach	Marnoch	5	9
SIM	Elizabeth	43	Botriphnie	Marnoch	5	9
SIM	Elizabeth	22	Culsalmond ABD	Marnoch	3	17
SIM	Elspet	1mth	Marnoch	Marnoch	1	4
SIM	Findlater	18	Culsalmond ABD	Marnoch	3	17
SIM	George	2	Marnoch	Marnoch	5	10
SIM	George	2	Marnoch	Marnoch	8	3
SIM	Helen	4	Marnoch	Marnoch	5	10

SURNAME	CHR. NAME	AGE	BIRTH PLACE	CENSUS PARISH	BOOK	PG
SIM	Isabel	9	Marnoch	Marnoch	5	10
SIM	James	1mth	Marnoch	Marnoch	8	3
SIM	James	16	Mortlach	Marnoch	9	2
SIM	James	47	Tarves ABD	Marnoch	5	9
SIM	Jane	43	Inverkeithny	Inverkeithny	1	5
SIM	Janet	74	Alvah	Marnoch	5	23
SIM	Jean	1	Marnoch	Marnoch	1	4
SIM	John	17	Cairnie ABD	Marnoch	3	12
SIM	John	25	Alvah	Forglen	4	7
SIM	John	57	Turriff ABD	Forglen	1	4
SIM	Margaret	28	Elgin MOR	Marnoch	8	5
SIM	Margaret	69	Marnoch	Inverkeithny	2	18
SIM	William	5	Marnoch	Marnoch	8	3
SIM	William	39	Culsalmond ABD	Marnoch	8	3
SIM	William	13	Mortlach	Marnoch	9	2
SIM	William	69	Culsalmond ABD	Marnoch	3	17
SIM	William	48	Auchterless ABD	Inverkeithny	1	5
SIMPSON	Alexander	74	Cairnie ABD	Marnoch	2	8
SIMPSON	Alexander	14	Marnoch	Marnoch	2	9
SIMPSON	Alexander	58	Marnoch	Marnoch	8	1
SIMPSON	Alexander	19	Marnoch	Marnoch	8	1
SIMPSON	Alexander	4	Marnoch	Marnoch	9	7
SIMPSON	Andrew	59	Marnoch	Inverkeithny	3	10
SIMPSON	Ann	11	Inverkeithny	Marnoch	8	5
SIMPSON	Betty	22	Marnoch	Marnoch	7	15
SIMPSON	Elizabeth	28	Rathven	Marnoch	6	10
SIMPSON	Elizabeth	30	Marnoch	Marnoch	8	4
SIMPSON	Elspet	28	Inverkeithny	Inverkeithny	2	6
SIMPSON	Elspet	17	Marnoch	Marnoch	8	1
SIMPSON	George	9	Marnoch	Marnoch	8	6
SIMPSON	George	31	Marnoch	Inverkeithny	3	10
SIMPSON	George	2	Inverkeithny	Inverkeithny	3	10
SIMPSON	George	39	Rothiemay	Marnoch	2	8
SIMPSON	George	44	Rothiemay	Marnoch	8	5
SIMPSON	Helen	16	Marnoch	Marnoch	9	7
SIMPSON	Helen	32	Marnoch	Marnoch	7	15
SIMPSON	Isabel	21	Marnoch	Marnoch	9	7
SIMPSON	Isabella	30	Rothiemay	Marnoch	2	9
SIMPSON	Isabella	25	Marnoch	Marnoch	8	1
SIMPSON	Isabella	6	Grange	Marnoch	2	9
SIMPSON	Isobel	80	Marnoch	Marnoch	2	11
SIMPSON	James	4	Inverkeithny	Inverkeithny	3	10
SIMPSON	James	36	Inverkeithny	Inverkeithny	2	6
SIMPSON	James	50	Marnoch	Marnoch	9	6
SIMPSON	James	64	Marnoch	Marnoch	8	4
SIMPSON	James	13	Inverkeithny	Marnoch	8	10
SIMPSON	James	17	Monquhitter ABD	Marnoch	8	8
SIMPSON	Jane	48	Cairnie ABD	Marnoch	9	6
SIMPSON	Jane	4	Keith	Marnoch	7	13
SIMPSON	Janet	36	Cullen	Marnoch	8	5
SIMPSON	Jean	25	Marnoch	Marnoch	8	2
SIMPSON	John	26	Marnoch	Inverkeithny	3	4
SIMPSON	John	73	Keith	Marnoch	7	15
SIMPSON	John	18	Marnoch	Marnoch	8	4
SIMPSON	Margaret	33	Inverkeithny	Inverkeithny	3	10
SIMPSON	Margaret	60	Auchterless ABD	Inverkeithny	3	3
SIMPSON	Margaret	63	Rothiemay	Marnoch	2	8
SIMPSON	Margaret	62	Marnoch	Marnoch	8	4
SIMPSON	Margaret	3	Inverkeithny	Inverkeithny	3	11
SIMPSON	Margaret	29	Marnoch	Marnoch	6	14
SIMPSON	Margaret	79	Forgue ABD	Marnoch	5	12
SIMPSON	Margaret	76	Forglen	Marnoch	1	2
SIMPSON	Mary	6	Marnoch	Marnoch	8	6
SIMPSON	Mary	28	Rothiemay	Inverkeithny	3	10

SURNAME	CHR. NAME	AGE	BIRTH PLACE	CENSUS PARISH	BOOK	PG
SIMPSON	Peter	31	Inverkeithny	Inverkeithny	2	6
SIMPSON	William	31	Rothiemay	Marnoch	2	8
SIMPSON	William	18	Marnoch	Marnoch	8	6
SIMPSON	William	65	Banff	Inverkeithny	2	6
SINCLAIR	Christian	50	Forgue ABD	Marnoch	1	12
SINCLAIR	Helen	53	Marnoch	Marnoch	4	10
SINCLAIR	Jane	19	Marnoch	Marnoch	2	1
SINCLAIR	Joseph	38	Strichen ABD	Marnoch	2	5
SINCLAIR	Mary	56	Marnoch	Marnoch	4	10
SINCLAIR	Mary	15	Inveravon	Marnoch	2	2
SISIEVERIGHT	Mary	16	Marnoch	Marnoch	6	6
SIVERIGHT	Anne	7	Marnoch	Marnoch	3	11
SIVERIGHT	Elizabeth	3	Marnoch	Marnoch	3	11
SIVERIGHT	George	9	Marnoch	Marnoch	3	11
SIVERIGHT	George	50	Canada	Marnoch	3	11
SIVERIGHT	Jane	39	Huntly ABD	Marnoch	3	11
SIVERIGHT	John	5	Marnoch	Marnoch	3	11
SKEEN	Elspet	80	Marnoch	Marnoch	7	5
SKEEN	Helen	40	Marnoch	Marnoch	7	5
SKEEN	John	81	Marnoch	Marnoch	7	5
SKENE	Alexander	52	Ordiquhill	Marnoch	2	11
SKENE	Alexander	73	Marnoch	Marnoch	3	9
SKENE	Elspet	60	Fintray ABD	Marnoch	5	22
SKENE	Mary	60	Auchterless ABD	Marnoch	3	9
SKINNER	Jean	70	Huntly ABD	Marnoch	9	5
SLORACH	William	61	Inverkeithny	Inverkeithny	3	14
SMALL	Andrew	46	Turriff ABD	Marnoch	3	7
SMALL	Anne	15	Marnoch	Marnoch	3	7
SMALL	Isobel	18	Marnoch	Marnoch	3	7
SMALL	Jane	50	Marnoch	Marnoch	3	7
SMALL	William	1	Marnoch	Marnoch	3	7
SMART	Alexander	15	Auchterless ABD	Marnoch	8	9
SMART	Barbara	4	Marnoch	Marnoch	6	27
SMART	Catherine	8	Marnoch	Marnoch	6	27
SMART	Christian	30	Inverkeithny	Inverkeithny	2	7
SMART	Clementina	5	Forgue ABD	Marnoch	5	25
SMART	Elizabeth	9	Monquhitter ABD	Marnoch	5	25
SMART	Elspet	69	Turriff ABD	Inverkeithny	2	7
SMART	James	74	Turriff ABD	Inverkeithny	2	6
SMART	James	31	Turriff ABD	Inverkeithny	3	10
SMART	Jane	23	Cabrach	Inverkeithny	3	2
SMART	Janet	5	Marnoch	Marnoch	1	3
SMART	John	2	Marnoch	Marnoch	5	25
SMART	Joseph	7	Turriff ABD	Marnoch	5	25
SMART	Margaret	12	Forgue ABD	Marnoch	5	25
SMART	Margaret	18	Cabrach	Inverkeithny	3	1
SMART	Peter	40	Turriff ABD	Marnoch	5	25
SMART	William	29	Marnoch	Marnoch	9	10
SMITH	Agnes	61	Strichen ABD	Marnoch	6	19
SMITH	Alexander	55	Forglen	Forglen	1	3
SMITH	Alexander	40	Chapel of Garioch ABD	Inverkeithny	2	7
SMITH	Alexander	8	Inverkeithny	Inverkeithny	2	10
SMITH	Alexander	7	Inverkeithny	Inverkeithny	3	3
SMITH	Alexander	13	Rothiemay	Marnoch	3	1
SMITH	Alexander	36	Forglen	Marnoch	8	3
SMITH	Alexander	73	Marnoch	Marnoch	3	7
SMITH	Alexander	57	Turriff ABD	Marnoch	3	3
SMITH	Andrew	66	Banff	Forglen	4	2
SMITH	Andrew	3	Marnoch	Marnoch	6	15
SMITH	Ann	40	Alvah	Forglen	2	4
SMITH	Ann	34	Fordyce	Marnoch	4	11
SMITH	Barbara	68	Drumblade ABD	Marnoch	6	6
SMITH	Charles	34	Marnoch	Marnoch	5	2
SMITH	Charles	7	Marnoch	Marnoch	6	26

SURNAME	CHR. NAME	AGE	BIRTH PLACE	CENSUS PARISH	BOOK	PG
SMITH	Charles	19	Marnoch	Inverkeithny	1	3
SMITH	Charles	31	Fordyce	Marnoch	4	11
SMITH	Elizabeth	4	Inverkeithny	Inverkeithny	2	7
SMITH	Elspet	30	Alvah	Inverkeithny	2	4
SMITH	Elspet	66	King Edward ABD	Marnoch	8	3
SMITH	George	82	Cairnie ABD	Marnoch	4	14
SMITH	George	16	Rothiemay	Marnoch	3	1
SMITH	George	10	Inverkeithny	Inverkeithny	2	10
SMITH	George	10mths	Marnoch	Marnoch	6	14
SMITH	George	12	Marnoch	Marnoch	3	7
SMITH	George	44	Chapel of Garioch ABD	Inverkeithny	2	12
SMITH	George Rannie	3mths	Forglen	Forglen	2	4
SMITH	Helen	35	Rayne ABD	Inverkeithny	2	7
SMITH	Helen	16	Auchterless ABD	Inverkeithny	2	10
SMITH	Helen	34	Rothes MOR	Inverkeithny	2	1
SMITH	Isabel	12	Inverkeithny	Inverkeithny	2	4
SMITH	Isabel	47	Rothiemay	Marnoch	6	26
SMITH	Isabella	55	Inverkeithny	Forglen	1	3
SMITH	Isabella	60	Rathen? ABD	Marnoch	3	16
SMITH	Isabella	7mths	Marnoch	Marnoch	4	9
SMITH	Isobel	31	Marnoch	Marnoch	1	11
SMITH	James	25	Forglen	Forglen	1	3
SMITH	James	7	Inverkeithny	Inverkeithny	2	4
SMITH	James	4	Inverkeithny	Inverkeithny	3	3
SMITH	James	35	Daviot ABD	Marnoch	1	11
SMITH	James	48	Gartly ABD	Marnoch	7	11
SMITH	James	13	Marnoch	Marnoch	6	26
SMITH	James	11	Marnoch	Marnoch	1	11
SMITH	James	38	Drumblade ABD	Inverkeithny	2	4
SMITH	James	56	Marnoch	Marnoch	6	14
SMITH	Jane	47	Leochel ABD	Marnoch	7	11
SMITH	Janet	72	Marnoch	Marnoch	3	7
SMITH	Jean	27	Oyne ABD	Inverkeithny	2	11
SMITH	Jessie	17	Marnoch	Marnoch	6	26
SMITH	Jessie	27	Marnoch	Marnoch	3	7
SMITH	John	35	Forgue ABD	Forglen	2	5
SMITH	John	50	Kintore ABD	Marnoch	3	11
SMITH	John	75	Marnoch	Marnoch	8	3
SMITH	John	31	Marnoch	Marnoch	1	13
SMITH	John	31	Forglen	Inverkeithny	3	3
SMITH	Margaret	33	Marnoch	Marnoch	1	2
SMITH	Margaret	70	Marnoch	Marnoch	4	11
SMITH	Margaret	34	Rothiemay	Inverkeithny	3	3
SMITH	Margaret	47	Rothiemay	Inverkeithny	2	4
SMITH	Margaret	1	Inverkeithny	Inverkeithny	2	5
SMITH	Mary	18	Edinburgh MLN	Forglen	2	9
SMITH	Mary	42	Auchterless ABD	Inverkeithny	2	10
SMITH	Mary	51	Cairnie ABD	Marnoch	4	14
SMITH	Mary	14	Auchterless ABD	Inverkeithny	2	10
SMITH	Mary	70	Banff	Marnoch	5	22
SMITH	Peter	11?	Inverkeithny	Inverkeithny	2	10
SMITH	Peter	37	Turriff ABD	Inverkeithny	2	10
SMITH	Robert	24	Alvah	Inverkeithny	2	4
SMITH	Robert	10	Marnoch	Marnoch	3	7
SMITH	Robert	23	Oyne ABD	Inverkeithny	2	11
SMITH	William	83	Aberdour? ABD	Forglen	2	4
SMITH	William	21	Forglen	Forglen	1	3
SMITH	William	22	Alvah	Marnoch	7	7
SMITH	William	2	Marnoch	Marnoch	2	13
SMITH	William	43	Marnoch	Marnoch	6	26
SMITH	William	15	Rothiemay	Marnoch	6	11
SMITH	female	3mths	Inverkeithny	Inverkeithny	2	11
SMOLLET	George	35	Alvah	Forglen	3	5
SMOLLET	John	38	Alvah	Inverkeithny	2	4

SURNAME	CHR. NAME	AGE	BIRTH PLACE	CENSUS PARISH	BOOK	PG
SMOLLET	Rebecca	40	Banff	Forglen	3	5
SOUTTER	David	14	Marnoch	Marnoch	1	1
SPENCE	Ann	13	Marnoch	Marnoch	2	14
SPENCE	Ann	42	Boharm	Marnoch	2	14
SPENCE	Elspet	52	Inverkeithny	Marnoch	8	9
SPENCE	George	30	Forglen	Forglen	1	5
SPENCE	Jean	23	Deskford	Forglen	2	10
SPENCE	Jean	7	Monquhitter ABD	Forglen	2	10
SPENCE	John	73	Inverkeithny	Forglen	1	3
SPENCE	John	3	Keith	Forglen	2	10
SPENCE	John	16	Marnoch	Inverkeithny	3	4
SPENCE	John	34	Forglen	Marnoch	8	9
SPENCE	Margaret	23	Marnoch	Forglen	3	6
SPENCE	Margaret	69	Forglen	Forglen	1	3
SPENCE	Margaret	7	Marnoch	Marnoch	2	14
SPENCE	Margaret	28	Rhynie ABD	Inverkeithny	2	2
SPENCE	Robert	25	Forglen	Forglen	2	10
SPENCE	Robert	4	Marnoch	Marnoch	2	14
SPENCE	William	1	Forglen	Forglen	2	10
SPENCE	William	41	Forglen	Marnoch	2	14
SPENCE	William	11	Marnoch	Marnoch	2	14
STABLES	Ann	1	Marnoch	Marnoch	5	25
STABLES	Archibald	36	Marnoch	Marnoch	6	7
STABLES	Archibald	2	Marnoch	Marnoch	6	7
STABLES	Jane	12	Marnoch	Marnoch	6	26
STABLES	Margaret	26	Marnoch	Marnoch	5	6
STABLES	Mary	26	Huntly ABD	Marnoch	6	7
STABLES	Mary	11mths	Marnoch	Marnoch	6	7
STABLES	William	70	Marnoch	Marnoch	5	6
STALKER	Mary	15	Marnoch	Marnoch	5	4
STEINSON	Elspet	23	Fordyce	Marnoch	3	12
STEPHAN	Elizabeth	5	Marnoch	Marnoch	4	3
STEPHAN	Elizabeth M.	33	Marnoch	Marnoch	4	3
STEPHAN	Elspet	1	Marnoch	Marnoch	4	3
STEPHAN	James	31	Culsalmond ABD	Marnoch	4	3
STEPHAN	Janet	7	Marnoch	Marnoch	4	3
STEPHEN	Alexander	1	Marnoch	Marnoch	4	5
STEPHEN	Ann	5	Marnoch	Marnoch	4	5
STEPHEN	David	7	Marnoch	Marnoch	4	5
STEPHEN	Elizabeth	20	Forgue ABD	Marnoch	8	4
STEPHEN	George	28	Culsalmond ABD	Marnoch	3	17
STEPHEN	George	4	Marnoch	Marnoch	4	5
STEPHEN	James	36	Turriff ABD	Marnoch	4	5
STEPHEN	James	12	Huntly ABD	Marnoch	4	5
STEPHEN	James	3	Monquhitter ABD	Marnoch	3	17
STEPHEN	Jane	23	Culsalmond ABD	Marnoch	3	17
STEPHEN	Jane E.	1	Marnoch	Marnoch	3	17
STEPHEN	John	13	Insch ABD	Marnoch	2	13
STEPHEN	Mary	32	Cairnie ABD	Marnoch	4	5
STEPHEN	Mary	9	Huntly ABD	Marnoch	4	5
STEPHEN	Robert	40	Inverness INV	Inverkeithny	2	12
STEPHEN	William	3mths	Marnoch	Marnoch	3	17
STEPHEN	William	20	Oyne ABD	Inverkeithny	1	1
STEVENSON	Alexander	58	Forglen	Forglen	2	3
STEVENSON	Alexander	3mths	Marnoch	Marnoch	2	13
STEVENSON	Alexander	22	Boyndie	Marnoch	2	13
STEVENSON	Elizabeth	61	Forglen	Forglen	2	6
STEVENSON	Isabella	25	Keith	Marnoch	2	13
STEVENSON	James	43	Forglen	Forglen	2	6
STEVENSON	John	35	Forglen	Forglen	2	11
STEVENSON	Margaret	53	Turriff ABD	Forglen	2	3
STEVENSON	Margaret	19	Forglen	Forglen	2	3
STEVENSON?	Robert	67	Boyndie	Marnoch	5	20
STEWART	Alexander	8	Marnoch	Marnoch	6	3

SURNAME	CHR. NAME	AGE	BIRTH PLACE	CENSUS PARISH	BOOK	PG
STEWART	Alexander	3	Forglen	Marnoch	5	1
STEWART	Alexander	30	Forglen	Marnoch	5	1
STEWART	Alexander	20	Mortlach	Marnoch	1	13
STEWART	Andrew	21	Turriff ABD	Marnoch	8	2
STEWART	Ann	26	Strathdon ABD	Forglen	1	5
STEWART	Ann	1	Forglen	Marnoch	5	1
STEWART	Charles	20	Forglen	Forglen	3	1
STEWART	Charles	57	Mortlach	Marnoch	5	8
STEWART	Christian	28	Fordyce	Marnoch	3	8
STEWART	Christian	7	Marnoch	Marnoch	3	9
STEWART	Elizabeth	35'	Marnoch	Marnoch	6	4
STEWART	George	33	Forglen	Forglen	2	9
STEWART	George	4mths	Marnoch	Marnoch	3	9
STEWART	George	58	Marnoch	Marnoch	5	4
STEWART	George	29	Marnoch	Marnoch	3	8
STEWART	George	60	Alvah	Marnoch	8	2
STEWART	George	7	Marnoch	Marnoch	6	25
STEWART	Helen	26	Culsalmond ABD	Marnoch	6	7
STEWART	Helen	4	Forglen	Marnoch	5	1
STEWART	Isobel	1mth	Forglen	Marnoch	6	25
STEWART	James	2	Marnoch	Marnoch	6	25
STEWART	James	59	Marnoch	Marnoch	3	9
STEWART	James	5	Marnoch	Marnoch	3	9
STEWART	James	36	Culsalmond ABD	Marnoch	6	7
STEWART	Jane	72	Turriff ABD	Forglen	4	3
STEWART	Jane	63	Marnoch	Marnoch	6	5
STEWART	Jean	14	Marnoch	Marnoch	5	8
STEWART	Jean	9	Marnoch	Marnoch	6	25
STEWART	Jean	4	Marnoch	Marnoch	5	25
STEWART	Margaret	51	Auchterless ABD	Marnoch	8	2
STEWART	Margaret	24	Culsalmond ABD	Marnoch	6	7
STEWART	Margaret	7	Marnoch	Marnoch	6	11
STEWART	Mary	27	Cuminestown ABD	Marnoch	6	18
STEWART	William	64	Alvah	Forglen	4	3
STEWART	William	4mths	Marnoch	Marnoch	6	25
STRACHAN	Alexander	26	Crimond ABD	Forglen	1	7
STRACHAN	Elizabeth	6	Inverkeithny	Inverkeithny	2	8
STRACHAN	Elizabeth	56	King Edward ABD	Marnoch	2	9
STRACHAN	George	36	Fordyce	Forglen	1	9
STRACHAN	Isabella	11	Ordiquhill	Marnoch	2	13
STRACHAN	Isabella	44	Alvah	Inverkeithny	2	8
STRACHAN	Isabella	45	Daviot ABD	Marnoch	2	13
STRACHAN	James	13	Inverkeithny	Inverkeithny	2	7
STRACHAN	Jane	16	Ordiquhill	Marnoch	2	10
STRACHAN	Jean	2	Inverkeithny	Inverkeithny	2	8
STRACHAN	John	39	Fyvie ABD	Inverkeithny	2	8
STRACHAN	John	18	Alvah	Inverkeithny	2	8
STRACHAN	John	54	Fordyce	Marnoch	2	9
STRACHAN	Mary	15	Alvah	Inverkeithny	2	7
STRACHAN	William	8	Ordiquhill	Marnoch	2	14
STRACHAN	William	24	Turriff ABD	Marnoch	2	9
STRACHAN	William	11	Inverkeithny	Inverkeithny	2	9
STRONACH	Ann	49	Banff	Marnoch	1	12
STRONACH	William	55	New Machar ABD	Marnoch	1	12
STUART	Alexander	1	Marnoch	Marnoch	9	5
STUART	Ann	60	Inveravon	Marnoch	2	4
STUART	Charles	9	Marnoch	Marnoch	2	4
STUART	Charles	39	Mortlach	Marnoch	2	4
STUART	Daniel	20	Fordyce	Marnoch	2	4
STUART	Grace	22	Abernethy INV	Marnoch	2	4
STUART	James	13	Inveravon	Marnoch	2	4
STUART	James	12	Marnoch	Marnoch	2	4
STUART	Jane	7	Marnoch	Marnoch	2	4
STUART	Jane	39	Aberlour	Marnoch	2	4

SURNAME	CHR. NAME	AGE	BIRTH PLACE	CENSUS PARISH	BOOK	PG
STUART	Jane	36	Inveravon	Marnoch	2	2
STUART	Janet	3	Marnoch	Marnoch	2	4
STUART	John	16	Inveravon	Marnoch	2	3
STUART	John	1mth	Marnoch	Marnoch	2	4
STUART	John D.	25	Errol PER	Marnoch	2	7
STUART	Margaret	8	Marnoch	Marnoch	1	2
STUART	Mary	5	Marnoch	Marnoch	2	4
STUART	Paul	47	Inveravon	Marnoch	2	6
STUART	Peter	30	Inveravon	Marnoch	2	3
STUART	Robert	62	Inveravon	Marnoch	2	4
STUART	William	28	Inveravon	Marnoch	2	2
STUART	William	14	Mortlach	Marnoch	2	4
SUMER	William	34	Birse ABD	Forglen	3	8
SUTHERLAND	Catherine	82	Loth SUT	Marnoch	7	10
SUTHERLAND	James	6	Keith	Marnoch	7	11
SUTHERLAND	Margaret	8	Marnoch	Marnoch	5	11
SYMON	Alexander	22	Deskford	Marnoch	1	10
SYMON	Ann	3	Inveravon	Marnoch	5	14
SYMON	George	13	Rothiemay	Marnoch	5	14
SYMON	Isobel	64	Marnoch	Marnoch	6	1
SYMON	Janet	40	Duffus MOR	Marnoch	5	14
SYMON	Jessie	15	Rothiemay	Marnoch	3	13
SYMON	John	38	Elgin MOR	Marnoch	5	14
SYMON	Margaret	11	Rothiemay	Marnoch	5	14
SYMON	Mary	38	Ordiquhill	Marnoch	5	19
TAIT	John	32	Culsalmond ABD	Marnoch	9	7
TARNAY	John	23	Augheboy MOG IRL	Inverkeithny	1	3
TARVES	George	16	Marnoch	Marnoch	3	10
TAWS	Alexander	24	Turriff ABD	Marnoch	4	13
TAWSE	Ann	5mths	Marnoch	Marnoch	9	10
TAYLOR	Alexander	20	Ordiquhill	Marnoch	5	10
TAYLOR	Alexander	36	Marnoch	Marnoch	5	8
TAYLOR	Alexander	11	Forglen	Forglen	4	10
TAYLOR	Alexander	30	Banff	Marnoch	3	5
TAYLOR	Alexander	44	Forgue ABD	Marnoch	2	8
TAYLOR	Alexander	3	Marnoch	Marnoch	3	7
TAYLOR	Alexander	39	Ordiquhill	Marnoch	3	7
TAYLOR	Ann	6	Marnoch	Marnoch	2	3
TAYLOR	Ann	43	Gamrie	Forglen	4	10
TAYLOR	Ann	63	Fordyce	Marnoch	5	15
TAYLOR	Ann	35	Aberlour	Marnoch	2	3
TAYLOR	Ann	43	Boyndie	Marnoch	2	1
TAYLOR	Ann	5	Marnoch	Marnoch	3	5
TAYLOR	Ann	17	Forglen	Forglen	4	10
TAYLOR	Anne	22	Marnoch	Marnoch	3	6
TAYLOR	Anne	32	Marnoch	Marnoch	3	5
TAYLOR	Charles	24	Ordiquhill	Marnoch	5	10
TAYLOR	Charles	50	Ordiquhill	Marnoch	2	3
TAYLOR	Christian	37	Banff	Marnoch	5	18
TAYLOR	Christian	5	Marnoch	Marnoch	2	1
TAYLOR	Constance A.	5	Forglen	Forglen	1	6
TAYLOR	David	1mth	Forglen	Forglen	1	1
TAYLOR	David	47	Forglen	Forglen	1	1
TAYLOR	Eliza	19	Ordiquhill	Forglen	3	2
TAYLOR	Elizabeth	15	New Deer ABD	Forglen	1	6
TAYLOR	Elizabeth	7	Forglen	Forglen	4	10
TAYLOR	Elizabeth	8	Marnoch	Marnoch	3	5
TAYLOR	Elsie Wilson	8	Marnoch	Marnoch	5	8
TAYLOR	Elspet	15	Ordiquhill	Marnoch	7	15
TAYLOR	Elspet	47	Fordyce	Marnoch	1	4
TAYLOR	Elspet	10	Marnoch	Marnoch	2	3
TAYLOR	Elspet	68	Marnoch	Marnoch	6	22
TAYLOR	Ernest	1	Marnoch	Marnoch	3	5
TAYLOR	Ernest	64	Ordiquhill	Forglen	3	2

SURNAME	CHR. NAME	AGE	BIRTH PLACE	CENSUS PARISH	BOOK	PG
TAYLOR	George	22	Marnoch	Marnoch	6	22
TAYLOR	George	70	Marnoch	Marnoch	5	22
TAYLOR	George	46	Forglen	Forglen	1	1
TAYLOR	George	5	Forglen	Forglen	4	10
TAYLOR	George	36	Ordiquhill	Marnoch	3	6
TAYLOR	George	13	Marnoch	Marnoch	2	8
TAYLOR	George	9mths	Forglen	Forglen	3	3
TAYLOR	George	28	Turriff ABD	Forglen	2	9
TAYLOR	Georgie Al.	8	Forglen	Forglen	1	6
TAYLOR	Harriet	31	Forgue ABD	Forglen	4	1
TAYLOR	Harriet C.	4	Forglen	Forglen	4	1
TAYLOR	Helen	1	Marnoch	Marnoch	5	18
TAYLOR	Isabel	28	Marnoch	Marnoch	5	18
TAYLOR	Isabel	68	Forgue ABD	Marnoch	5	25
TAYLOR	Isabella	49	Alford ABD	Forglen	3	2
TAYLOR	Isabella	8	Marnoch	Marnoch	2	3
TAYLOR	James	65	Marnoch	Marnoch	1	2
TAYLOR	James	41	Ordiquhill	Marnoch	2	1
TAYLOR	James	64	Marnoch	Marnoch	6	22
TAYLOR	James	3	Marnoch	Marnoch	5	9
TAYLOR	James	2	Marnoch	Marnoch	5	4
TAYLOR	James	7	Marnoch	Marnoch	4	5
TAYLOR	James	1	Marnoch	Marnoch	3	7
TAYLOR	James	11	Marnoch	Marnoch	1	4
TAYLOR	James	14	Inveravon	Marnoch	9	10
TAYLOR	James	40	Forglen	Forglen	4	10
TAYLOR	James	23	Ordiquhill	Inverkeithny	3	12
TAYLOR	James	1	Marnoch	Marnoch	2	3
TAYLOR	Jane	11mths	Marnoch	Marnoch	5	9
TAYLOR	Jane	35	Ellon ABD	Forglen	1	6
TAYLOR	Jane	38	Marnoch	Forglen	1	1
TAYLOR	Jane	3	Marnoch	Marnoch	2	3
TAYLOR	Jean	7mths	Forglen	Forglen	1	6
TAYLOR	Jean	19	Marnoch	Marnoch	8	10
TAYLOR	Jessie	5	Marnoch	Marnoch	5	9
TAYLOR	John	47	Tarves ABD	Marnoch	1	4
TAYLOR	John	30	Forgue ABD	Inverkeithny	3	6
TAYLOR	John	45	Forglen	Forglen	4	1
TAYLOR	John	3	Forglen	Forglen	4	10
TAYLOR	John	46	Marnoch	Forglen	1	1
TAYLOR	John	5	Auchterless ABD	Marnoch	5	24
TAYLOR	John	38	Edinburgh MLN	Marnoch	5	24
TAYLOR	John	10	Marnoch	Marnoch	3	5
TAYLOR	John	2	Marnoch	Marnoch	5	18
TAYLOR	John	16	Ordiquhill	Marnoch	5	10
TAYLOR	John	47	Ordiquhill	Marnoch	5	18
TAYLOR	John Cameron	2	Boyndie	Forglen	3	2
TAYLOR	Joseph	22	Ordiquhill	Marnoch	8	5
TAYLOR	Lauchlan	20	Ordiquhill	Forglen	3	2
TAYLOR	Lillias	52	Marnoch	Marnoch	5	10
TAYLOR	Margaret	25	Grange	Marnoch	3	7
TAYLOR	Margaret	24	King Edward ABD	Marnoch	5	24
TAYLOR	Margaret	14	Marnoch	Marnoch	2	8
TAYLOR	Margaret	37	Ordiquhill	Marnoch	2	8
TAYLOR	Margaret	21	Fyvie ABD	Forglen	2	10
TAYLOR	Mary	12	New Deer ABD	Forglen	1	6
TAYLOR	Mary	13	Ordiquhill	Marnoch	2	3
TAYLOR	Mary	55	Ordiquhill	Marnoch	3	10
TAYLOR	Mary	64	Banff	Marnoch	1	2
TAYLOR	Mary L.	3	Forglen	Forglen	4	1
TAYLOR	Robert	44	New Deer ABD	Forglen	1	6
TAYLOR	Robert	35	Aberdeen ABD	Marnoch	6	11
TAYLOR	Robert	3	Forglen	Forglen	1	6
TAYLOR	Susan B.	1	Forglen	Forglen	4	1

SURNAME	CHR. NAME	AGE	BIRTH PLACE	CENSUS PARISH	BOOK	PG
TAYLOR	William	6mths	Marnoch	Marnoch	3	6
TAYLOR	William	39	Kemnay ABD	Forglen	3	8
TAYLOR	William	9	Forglen	Forglen	4	10
TAYLOR	William	7wks	Marnoch	Marnoch	5	4
TAYLOR	William	5	Grange	Marnoch	3	7
TAYLOR	William	27	Boyndie	Marnoch	5	4
TAYLOR	William	19	Ordiquhill	Marnoch	5	9
TAYLOR	male	1mth	Forglen	Forglen	4	10
TENTY	Isabella	23	Aberdour ABD	Inverkeithny	3	9
TEUNON	Christian	21	Alvah	Marnoch	3	2
TEUNON	Elizabeth	54	King Edward ABD	Marnoch	3	2
TEUNON	James	48	Forglen	Marnoch	3	2
TEUNON	Robert	25	King Edward ABD	Marnoch	3	1
THAIN	Elizabeth	84	Forgie ABD	Marnoch	1	5
THAIN	Jane	67	Fordyce	Marnoch	3	4
THAIN	Mary	62	Fordyce	Marnoch	3	4
THAIN	William	7	Forglen	Forglen	4	3
THOM	Isabella	18	Rothiemay	Marnoch	1	14
THOM	James	25	Huntly ABD	Marnoch	6	20
THOM	James	9	Marnoch	Marnoch	3	9
THOM	Jean	30	Marnoch	Marnoch	6	20
THOMPSON	Adam	52	Marnoch	Marnoch	2	9
THOMPSON	Ann	80	Rothiemay	Marnoch	2	9
THOMPSON	Elizabeth	68	Marnoch	Marnoch	2	9
THOMPSON	Elizabeth	18	Marnoch	Marnoch	2	9
THOMPSON	George	25	Marnoch	Marnoch	2	7
THOMPSON	George	4	Rothiemay	Marnoch	2	8
THOMPSON	Helen	43	Ordiquhill	Marnoch	2	8
THOMPSON	James	70	Cairnie ABD	Marnoch	2	9
THOMPSON	James	10	Ordiquhill	Marnoch	2	8
THOMPSON	James	23	Gamrie	Inverkeithny	1	4
THOMPSON	Jane	21	Forglen	Forglen	1	8
THOMPSON	Jane	4	Marnoch	Marnoch	2	9
THOMPSON	Jessie	16	Lumphanan ABD	Inverkeithny	2	4
THOMPSON	Margaret	68	Inverkeithny	Inverkeithny	1	1
THOMPSON	William	81	Cairnie ABD	Marnoch	2	9
THOMSON	Alexander	14	Inverkeithny	Inverkeithny	3	6
THOMSON	Alexander	13	Ordiquhill	Marnoch	1	1
THOMSON	Alexander	24	Elgin MOR	Marnoch	5	12
THOMSON	Alexander	29	Marnoch	Forglen	1	9
THOMSON	Alexander	9	Ordiquhill	Marnoch	2	2
THOMSON	Ann	12	Inverkeithny	Inverkeithny	3	6
THOMSON	Ann	38	Inverkeithny	Inverkeithny	3	6
THOMSON	Ann	12	Forglen	Marnoch	1	5
THOMSON	Ann	22	Turriff ABD	Marnoch	5	12
THOMSON	Ann	20	Keith	Marnoch	5	11
THOMSON	Ann	20	Rothiemay	Forglen	4	4
THOMSON	Barbara	63	Forgue ABD	Marnoch	1	7
THOMSON	Barbra	13	Forgue ABD	Marnoch	5	20
THOMSON	Bell	20	Inverkeithny	Inverkeithny	3	7
THOMSON	Catherine	31	Marnoch	Marnoch	1	7
THOMSON	Charles	62	Marnoch	Marnoch	8	1
THOMSON	Charles	18	Marnoch	Marnoch	8	1
THOMSON	Elspet	4	Cairnie BAN	Marnoch	7	10
THOMSON	Elspet	42	Mortlach	Marnoch	7	10
THOMSON	George	12	Marnoch	Marnoch	5	11
THOMSON	George	4	Huntly ABD	Inverkeithny	3	7
THOMSON	George	21	Marnoch	Marnoch	5	18
THOMSON	George	18	Keith	Marnoch	8	6
THOMSON	George	22	Drumblade ABD	Forglen	3	3
THOMSON	George	14	Rothiemay	Marnoch	8	10
THOMSON	Hannah	30	Marnoch	Marnoch	9	10
THOMSON	Isabella	12	Bellie MOR	Forglen	3	1
THOMSON	Isabella	2	Cairnie BAN	Marnoch	7	10

SURNAME	CHR. NAME	AGE	BIRTH PLACE	CENSUS PARISH	BOOK	PG
THOMSON	James	49	Cairnie BAN	Marnoch	7	10
THOMSON	Jane	16	Kintore ABD	Forglen	4	7
THOMSON	Janet	67	Boyndie	Marnoch	4	14
THOMSON	Janet	55	Forgue ABD	Marnoch	5	9
THOMSON	Jean	48	Banff	Marnoch	5	4
THOMSON	Jean	60	Forgue ABD	Inverkeithny	3	7
THOMSON	Jean	17	Rothiemay	Forglen	3	1
THOMSON	Jessie	2	Fordyce	Marnoch	8	2
THOMSON	John	49	Banff	Marnoch	5	10
THOMSON	John	5	Marnoch	Marnoch	5	12
THOMSON	John	4mths	Marnoch	Marnoch	9	1
THOMSON	John	24	Forgue ABD	Forglen	2	7
THOMSON	John	71	Bellie MOR	Forglen	3	1
THOMSON	John	15	Rothiemay	Inverkeithny	3	8
THOMSON	John	12	Auchterless ABD	Forglen	2	5
THOMSON	Margaret	44	Keith	Marnoch	5	11
THOMSON	Margaret	57	Marnoch	Marnoch	8	1
THOMSON	Margaret	24	Marnoch	Marnoch	8	1
THOMSON	Margaret	35	Ordiquhill	Marnoch	2	2
THOMSON	Margaret	71	Urquhart MOR	Marnoch	9	10
THOMSON	Margaret	3	Inverkeithny	Inverkeithny	3	6
THOMSON	Mary	8mths	Boyndie	Marnoch	1	7
THOMSON	Mary	9	Cairnie BAN	Marnoch	7	10
THOMSON	Peter	11	Inverkeithny	Inverkeithny	3	6
THOMSON	Peter	49	Auchterless ABD	Inverkeithny	3	6
THOMSON	Robert	40	Aberdeen ABD	Marnoch	5	11
THOMSON	Robert	7	Cairnie BAN	Marnoch	7	10
THOMSON	Robert	66	Fetteresso KCD	Marnoch	5	12
THOMSON	Robert	86	Forglen	Marnoch	5	19
THOMSON	Robert	10	Marnoch	Marnoch	5	11
THOMSON	Robert	6	Marnoch	Marnoch	6	21
THOMSON	William	5	Ordiquhill	Marnoch	2	2
THOMSON	William	18	Rathven	Marnoch	8	5
THOMSON	William	5	Inverkeithny	Inverkeithny	3	6
THOW	Charles	13	Midmar ABD	Marnoch	4	13
THOW	Elizabeth	35	Midmar ABD	Marnoch	4	13
TOCHER	Alexander	24	Forgue ABD	Inverkeithny	2	14
TOCHER	Barbara	23	Insch ABD	Inverkeithny	2	14
TOCHER	George	61	Auchterless ABD	Marnoch	8	10
TOCHER	Helen	63	Midmar ABD	Inverkeithny	3	6
TOCHER	James	1	Auchterless ABD	Inverkeithny	2	14
TOCHER	Janet	63	Auchterless ABD	Marnoch	8	10
TOCHER	Jean	44	Forgue ABD	Marnoch	6	24
TOCHER	John	83	Fyvie ABD	Marnoch	6	24
TOCHER	Margaret	48	Marnoch	Marnoch	6	4
TOCHER	Mary	51	Boyndie	Marnoch	8	10
TOCHER	Peter	61	Auchterless ABD	Inverkeithny	3	6
TOCHER	Peter	22	Auchterless ABD	Inverkeithny	3	6
TODD	James	2	Marnoch	Marnoch	6	3
TORRIE	Alexander	68	Rayne ABD	Marnoch	5	11
TORRIE	Grace	62	Forglen	Forglen	2	4
TORRIE	Jane	30	Marnoch	Marnoch	5	11
TOUGH	Alexander	9	Rhynie ABD	Marnoch	4	12
TOUGH	Ann P.	1	Marnoch	Marnoch	4	12
TOUGH	Charles	3	Marnoch	Marnoch	4	12
TOUGH	David	44	Leslie ABD	Marnoch	4	12
TOUGH	David	12	Rhynie ABD	Marnoch	4	12
TOUGH	Elizabeth	8	Marnoch	Inverkeithny	3	8
TOUGH	Elspet	36	Leslie ABD	Marnoch	4	12
TOUGH	George	8	Rhynie ABD	Marnoch	4	12
TOUGH	Helen	6	Turriff ABD	Inverkeithny	3	9
TOUGH	James	16	Rhynie ABD	Marnoch	4	14
TOUGH	Jessie	40	Marnoch	Inverkeithny	3	8
TOUGH	John	6	Auchindoir ABD	Marnoch	4	12

SURNAME	CHR. NAME	AGE	BIRTH PLACE	CENSUS PARISH	BOOK	PG
TOUGH	Peter	1	Inverkeithny	Inverkeithny	3	9
TOUGH	William	16	Leslie ABD	Marnoch	4	12
TOUGH	William	42	Grange	Inverkeithny	2	10
TOUGH	William	11	Fordyce	Marnoch	2	8
TOUGH	William	3	Inverkeithny	Inverkeithny	3	9
TRAIL	Alexander	5mths	Marnoch	Marnoch	4	17
TRAIL	Alexander	29	Pitsligo ABD	Marnoch	4	17
TRAIL	Helen	10	Forgue ABD	Marnoch	4	9
TRAIL	Margaret	21	Forgue ABD	Marnoch	4	9
TRAIL	Mary	32	New Deer ABD	Marnoch	4	17
TRAIL	Mary	2	Tyrie ABD	Marnoch	4	17
TRAIL	Ratchel	50	Monquhitter ABD	Marnoch	4	9
TRAIL	William	50	King Edward ABD	Marnoch	4	9
TROUP	Alexander	8	Inverkeithny	Inverkeithny	3	11
TROUP	George	16	Inverkeithny	Inverkeithny	3	1
TROUP	Helen	6	Marnoch	Marnoch	5	13
TROUP	Isabella	15	Inverkeithny	Inverkeithny	3	3
TROUP	Isabella	37	Marnoch	Marnoch	5	7
TROUP	James	10	Inverkeithny	Inverkeithny	3	11
TROUP	Joseph	40	Udny ABD	Forglen	3	4
TROUP	Mary	21	Forglen	Forglen	3	4
TROUP	Mary Ann	2	Forglen	Forglen	3	4
TROUP	William	31	Udny ABD	Forglen	3	4
TROUP	William	5mths	Forglen	Forglen	3	4
TULLOCH	Ann	40	Grange	Marnoch	1	13
TULLOCH	John	20	Aberlour	Inverkeithny	2	12
TULLOCH	Margaret	31	Aberfeldy PER	Marnoch	6	12
URQUHART	Agnes	55	Drumblade ABD	Marnoch	4	16
URQUHART	Charles	46	Croy INV	Marnoch	4	16
URQUHART	Elizabeth	26	Turriff ABD	Forglen	2	7
URQUHART	James	16	Rothiemay	Marnoch	4	16
URQUHART	John	26	Marnoch	Marnoch	3	5
WALKER	Alexander	12	Marnoch	Marnoch	8	8
WALKER	Alexander	43	Marnoch	Marnoch	6	20
WALKER	Ann	45	Turriff ABD	Marnoch	6	19
WALKER	Anne	9	Marnoch	Marnoch	7	13
WALKER	Christian	72	Inverkeithny	Inverkeithny	1	1
WALKER	David	3	Marnoch	Marnoch	8	8
WALKER	Elizabeth	54	Inverkeithny	Marnoch	1	9
WALKER	Francis	31	Marnoch	Marnoch	8	5
WALKER	George	9	Inverkeithny	Inverkeithny	2	1
WALKER	Helen	45	Inverkeithny	Inverkeithny	2	6
WALKER	Helen	12	Marnoch	Marnoch	1	9
WALKER	Helen	8	Marnoch	Marnoch	8	7
WALKER	Helen	41	Banff	Forglen	2	6
WALKER	Helen	41	Banff	Forglen	2	6
WALKER	Isabel	16	Inverkeithny	Inverkeithny	3	12
WALKER	James	9	Inverkeithny	Inverkeithny	1	6
WALKER	James	14	Inverkeithny	Marnoch	4	6
WALKER	James	40	Inverkeithny	Inverkeithny	1	6
WALKER	Jane	83	Marnoch	Marnoch	6	28
WALKER	Janet	68	Turriff ABD	Marnoch	8	5
WALKER	Jean	58	Fyvie ABD	Marnoch	5	13
WALKER	John	3	Banff	Marnoch	7	13
WALKER	John	48	Banff	Marnoch	8	7
WALKER	John	4mths	Marnoch	Marnoch	5	8
WALKER	John	16	Marnoch	Marnoch	8	7
WALKER	Katherine	49	Marnoch	Inverkeithny	1	6
WALKER	Margaret	10	Marnoch	Marnoch	8	7
WALKER	Margaret	2	Marnoch	Marnoch	1	9
WALKER	Peter	29	Marnoch	Marnoch	1	9
WALKER	William	7	Marnoch	Marnoch	1	7
WALKER	William	14	Marnoch	Marnoch	8	5
WALLACE	Isabella	34	Marnoch	Inverkeithny	2	6

SURNAME	CHR. NAME	AGE	BIRTH PLACE	CENSUS PARISH	BOOK	PG
WALLACE	Robert	15	Kirkcolm WIG	Marnoch	4	8
WALLACE	William	33	Tyrie ABD	Inverkeithny	2	6
WATSON	Ann	34	Rathven	Marnoch	5	18
WATSON	Ann	11	Ordiquhill	Marnoch	2	13
WATSON	Elizabeth	43	Forgue ABD	Marnoch	2	13
WATSON	Elizabeth	34	Marnoch	Inverkeithny	3	8
WATSON	George	23	Marnoch	Marnoch	3	16
WATSON	George	72	Cairnie ABD	Marnoch	3	16
WATSON	George	16	Ordiquhill	Marnoch	2	13
WATSON	James	7	Marnoch	Marnoch	5	18
WATSON	James	12	Inverkeithny	Inverkeithny	2	10
WATSON	James	51	Fordyce	Marnoch	2	13
WATSON	Jane	17	Ordiquhill	Marnoch	2	13
WATSON	Jessie	19	Drumblade ABD	Inverkeithny	3	9
WATSON	John	26	Marnoch	Marnoch	3	16
WATSON	William	40	Marnoch	Inverkeithny	3	8
WATT	Alexander	12	Cairnie ABD	Marnoch	3	6
WATT	Alexander	1	Inverkeithny	Inverkeithny	3	5
WATT	Alexander M.	3mths	Marnoch	Marnoch	3	15
WATT	Ann	8	Alvah	Marnoch	7	10
WATT	Charles	40	Aberdeen ABD	Marnoch	1	1
WATT	Christina	21 days	Inverkeithny	Inverkeithny	3	5
WATT	Elizabeth	26	Forgue ABD	Inverkeithny	3	5
WATT	Elspet	73	Boyndie	Inverkeithny	1	4
WATT	Elspet	59	Fordyce	Marnoch	6	3
WATT	George	30	Auchterless ABD	Inverkeithny	3	5
WATT	George	49	Fordyce	Marnoch	8	8
WATT	Gordon	15	Ordiquhill	Marnoch	4	13
WATT	Helen	49	Cairnie ABD	Marnoch	3	6
WATT	James	22	Cairnie ABD	Marnoch	1	8
WATT	James	37	Glass ABD	Marnoch	3	15
WATT	James	1mth	Marnoch	Marnoch	1	8
WATT	James	21	Marnoch	Marnoch	3	12
WATT	Jane	18	Cairnie ABD	Marnoch	3	6
WATT	Jane	4	Inverkeithny	Inverkeithny	3	5
WATT	Jean	28	Marnoch	Marnoch	1	8
WATT	Jessie	27	Rothiemay	Marnoch	3	15
WATT	John	56	Marnoch	Marnoch	6	16
WATT	John	15	Cairnie ABD	Marnoch	3	6
WATT	Joseph	5	Forgue ABD	Inverkeithny	3	5
WATT	Mary	38	Aberdeen ABD	Marnoch	1	1
WATT	Nancy	34	Boyndie	Forglen	2	7
WATT	Nancy	34	Boyndie	Forglen	2	7
WATT	Robert	27	Cairnie ABD	Marnoch	3	6
WATT	Robert	14	Rothiemay	Marnoch	8	1
WATT	William	48	Boyndie	Forglen	2	7
WATT	William	7mths	Marnoch	Marnoch	5	16
WATT	William	21	Inverkeithny	Inverkeithny	2	12
WATT	William	63	Insch ABD	Inverkeithny	1	4
WATT	William	58	Cairnie ABD	Marnoch	3	6
WATT	Wm	48	Boyndie	Forglen	2	7
WATTIE	James	4	Turriff ABD	Inverkeithny	2	17
WATTIE	Jean	15	Inverkeithny	Marnoch	4	6
WEBSTER	Agnes	25	King Edward ABD	Forglen	2	5
WEBSTER	Agnes	25	King Edward ABD	Forglen	2	5
WEBSTER	Agnes	10?	Inverkeithny	Inverkeithny	1	1
WEBSTER	Alexander	2	Midmar ABD	Marnoch	4	16
WEBSTER	Alexander	59	Marnoch	Marnoch	9	7
WEBSTER	Ann	21	Forgue ABD	Inverkeithny	2	16
WEBSTER	Ann	63	Forglen	Forglen	2	2
WEBSTER	Ann	20	Forglen	Forglen	2	5
WEBSTER	Ann	63	Forglen	Forglen	2	2
WEBSTER	Ann	20	Forglen	Forglen	2	5
WEBSTER	Eliz.	18	Turriff ABD	Forglen	1	3

SURNAME	CHR. NAME	AGE	BIRTH PLACE	CENSUS PARISH	BOOK	PG
WEBSTER	Eliz.	17	Forglen	Forglen	2	5
WEBSTER	Elizabeth	67	Forgue ABD	Inverkeithny	2	16
WEBSTER	Elizabeth	17	Forglen	Forglen	2	5
WEBSTER	Elizabeth	18	Turriff ABD	Forglen	1	3
WEBSTER	Elspet	7	Marnoch	Marnoch	8	9
WEBSTER	Francis	21	Marnoch	Inverkeithny	3	15
WEBSTER	Geo	20	Forglen	Forglen	2	5
WEBSTER	Geo	54	Forglen	Forglen	2	5
WEBSTER	George	2	Marnoch	Marnoch	8	9
WEBSTER	George	54	Forglen	Forglen	2	5
WEBSTER	George	20	Forglen	Forglen	2	5
WEBSTER	George	57	Inverkeithny	Inverkeithny	3	10
WEBSTER	Helen	57	Marnoch	Marnoch	9	7
WEBSTER	Isabella	32	Rothiemay	Marnoch	6	25
WEBSTER	Isabella	50	Forglen	Forglen	3	3
WEBSTER	Isabella	50	Forglen	Forglen	3	3
WEBSTER	Isabella	27	King Edward ABD	Forglen	2	5
WEBSTER	Isabella	27	King Edward ABD	Forglen	2	5
WEBSTER	James	81	Marnoch	Forglen	3	3
WEBSTER	James	81	Marnoch	Forglen	3	3
WEBSTER	James	42	Forglen	Forglen	3	3
WEBSTER	James	33	Inverkeithny	Inverkeithny	1	3
WEBSTER	James	33	Midmar ABD	Marnoch	4	13
WEBSTER	James	42	Forglen	Forglen	3	3
WEBSTER	Jean	63	Forglen	Forglen	2	5
WEBSTER	Jean	63	Forglen	Forglen	2	5
WEBSTER	Jean	27	Marnoch	Marnoch	4	2
WEBSTER	Jean	19	Turriff ABD	Marnoch	8	9
WEBSTER	Jn	62	Marnoch	Forglen	2	5
WEBSTER	John	62	Marnoch	Forglen	2	5
WEBSTER	John	4	Marnoch	Marnoch	8	9
WEBSTER	Margaret	23	Forglen	Forglen	2	5
WEBSTER	Margaret	36	Turriff ABD	Marnoch	8	9
WEBSTER	Margt	23	Forglen	Forglen	2	5
WEBSTER	Mary	42	Forglen	Forglen	3	3
WEBSTER	Mary	51	Turriff ABD	Forglen	2	5
WEBSTER	Mary	42	Forglen	Forglen	3	3
WEBSTER	Mary	51	Turriff ABD	Forglen	2	5
WEBSTER	Robert	24	Monymusk ABD	Marnoch	9	4
WEBSTER	Robert	70	Marnoch	Marnoch	4	2
WEBSTER	Robert	19	Marnoch	Marnoch	4	2
WEBSTER	Robert	26	Udny ABD	Forglen	4	4
WEBSTER	Robert	26	Udny ABD	Forglen	4	4
WEBSTER	William	5	Marnoch	Marnoch	8	9
WEBSTER	William	66	Keith	Marnoch	6	12
WEBSTER	William	22	Turriff ABD	Forglen	3	8
WEBSTER	Wm	22	Turriff ABD	Forglen	3	8
WEIR	Geo	23	Cork IRL	Forglen	3	4
WEIR	George	23	Cork IRL	Forglen	3	4
WEIR	Jane	70	Marnoch	Marnoch	5	6
WHITE	Ann	14	Alvah	Inverkeithny	3	12
WHITE	Bathia	41	Alvah	Inverkeithny	3	12
WHITE	Bathia	12	Alvah	Inverkeithny	3	12
WHITE	Helen	10	Inverkeithny	Inverkeithny	3	12
WHITE	James	41	Marnoch	Inverkeithny	3	12
WHITE	James	7	Inverkeithny	Inverkeithny	3	12
WHITE	Jane	1	Inverkeithny	Inverkeithny	3	13
WHITE	John	3	Inverkeithny	Inverkeithny	3	13
WHITE	Margaret	72	Mortlach	Marnoch	7	9
WHITE	Margaret	18	Deskford	Inverkeithny	1	1
WHITE	William	5	Inverkcithny	Invcrkcithny	3	13
WHYTE	William	15	St Andrews-Llanbryde MOR	Marnoch	3	13
WILKIE	George	41	Keith	Inverkeithny	2	3
WILKIE	George	15	Rothiemay	Inverkeithny	2	3

SURNAME	CHR. NAME	AGE	BIRTH PLACE	CENSUS PARISH	BOOK	PG
WILKIE	Helen	7	Inverkeithny	Inverkeithny	2	3
WILLIAMS	Alexander	19	Gamrie	Marnoch	8	10
WILLIAMSON	Geo	31	Aberdeen ABD	Forglen	3	8
WILLIAMSON	Helen	32	Marnoch	Marnoch	5	20
WILLIAMSON	Janet	66	Forglen	Marnoch	5	20
WILLIAMSON	Jean	32	Aberdeen ABD	Forglen	3	8
WILLIAMSON	William	36	Blaekish? Cromarty	Inverkeithny	1	7
WILSON	Agnes	17	Marnoch	Marnoch	6	7
WILSON	Alex	9	Forglen	Forglen	4	8
WILSON	Alexander	4	Turriff ABD	Inverkeithny	2	16
WILSON	Alexander	12	Marnoch	Marnoch	7	5
WILSON	Alexander	50	Keith	Marnoch	9	9
WILSON	Alexander	44	Marnoch	Marnoch	3	15
WILSON	Alexander	5	Marnoch	Marnoch	3	16
WILSON	Andrew	21	Methlick ABD	Inverkeithny	3	12
WILSON	Ann	37	Banff	Marnoch	7	11
WILSON	Ann	7	Boyndie	Marnoch	7	1
WILSON	Ann	22	Forgue ABD	Inverkeithny	1	1
WILSON	Ann	1	Marnoch	Marnoch	5	10
WILSON	Ann	14	Marnoch	Inverkeithny	1	7
WILSON	Anne	51	Huntly ABD	Marnoch	7	5
WILSON	Catherine	35	Alvah	Marnoch	9	9
WILSON	David	1mth	Inverkeithny	Inverkeithny	2	16
WILSON	Elizabeth	40	Fyvie ABD	Inverkeithny	2	16
WILSON	Elizabeth	37	Forgue ABD	Marnoch	5	10
WILSON	Elspet	53	Banff	Forglen	2	2
WILSON	Elspet	17	Marnoch	Marnoch	4	2
WILSON	Elspet	66	Marnoch	Marnoch	7	13
WILSON	Garden(female)	23	Lumphanan ABD	Inverkeithny	2	4
WILSON	Hannah	2	Marnoch	Marnoch	3	16
WILSON	Helen	80	Fordyce	Marnoch	6	15
WILSON	Hester	50	Eastminster MDX	Marnoch	8	7
WILSON	Isabella	53	Marnoch	Marnoch	6	7
WILSON	James	22	Grange	Marnoch	4	8
WILSON	James	8	Marnoch	Marnoch	3	16
WILSON	James	36	Marnoch	Marnoch	5	21
WILSON	James	11	Marnoch	Marnoch	5	21
WILSON	James	15	Marnoch	Marnoch	6	7
WILSON	James	2	Marnoch	Marnoch	7	1
WILSON	James	27	Marnoch	Marnoch	7	14
WILSON	James	68	Marnoch	Marnoch	9	9
WILSON	James	24	Mintlaw ABD	Inverkeithny	2	4
WILSON	James	10	Turriff ABD	Inverkeithny	2	16
WILSON	Jane	21	Marnoch	Marnoch	7	5
WILSON	Jane	5	Marnoch	Marnoch	7	8
WILSON	Jane	10	Marnoch	Marnoch	3	16
WILSON	Jane	77	Grange	Marnoch	7	8
WILSON	Jane	68	Alvah	Marnoch	7	11
WILSON	Jane	4	Marnoch	Marnoch	5	10
WILSON	Jane	2	Marnoch	Marnoch	7	11
WILSON	Jessie	34	Marnoch	Marnoch	3	15
WILSON	Jessie	12	Marnoch	Marnoch	3	16
WILSON	Jessie	31	Ordiquhill	Marnoch	7	8
WILSON	John	10	Marnoch	Marnoch	5	10
WILSON	John	59	Boyndie	Marnoch	7	1
WILSON	John	9	Boyndie	Marnoch	7	1
WILSON	Laura	9	Alvah	Forglen	2	2
WILSON	Margaret	40	Marnoch	Marnoch	5	21
WILSON	Margaret	67	Boyndie	Marnoch	7	1
WILSON	Margaret	37	Dyke MOR	Marnoch	7	1
WILSON	Margaret D.	5	Marnoch	Marnoch	5	21
WILSON	Mary	42	Rothiemay	Marnoch	1	13
WILSON	Mary	37	Rothiemay	Marnoch	5	8
WILSON	Peter	13	Turriff ABD	Inverkeithny	2	16

SURNAME	CHR. NAME	AGE	BIRTH PLACE	CENSUS PARISH	BOOK	PG
WILSON	Peter	46	Marnoch	Marnoch	7	8
WILSON	Peter	55	Marnoch	Marnoch	6	7
WILSON	Peter	1	Marnoch	Marnoch	7	8
WILSON	Robert	6	Boyndie	Forglen	2	2
WILSON	Sarah	64	Turriff ABD	Marnoch	7	5
WILSON	William	50	Gamrie	Inverkeithny	2	16
WILSON	William	38	Marnoch	Marnoch	7	11
WILSON	William	9mths	Marnoch	Marnoch	7	11
WILSON	Wm	22	Methlick ABD	Forglen	4	4
WILSON	peter	86	Marnoch	Marnoch	7	8
WINTON	Ann	15	Alvah	Forglen	3	5
WINTON	Christina J.	1	Forglen	Forglen	4	9
WINTON	Elizabeth	46	Forglen	Marnoch	5	17
WINTON	Elizabeth	2	Forglen	Marnoch	9	11
WINTON	Francis	47	Forglen	Forglen	4	9
WINTON	George	54	Inverkeithny	Inverkeithny	2	10
WINTON	Helen	21	Inverkeithny	Inverkeithny	2	10
WINTON	Isabella	25	Edinburgh MID	Forglen	4	9
WINTON	James Fr.	1mth	Forglen	Forglen	4	9
WINTON	Janet	58	Inverkeithny	Inverkeithny	2	10
WINTON	John	47	Inverkeithny	Inverkeithny	2	10
WINTON	Joseph	24	Marnoch	Marnoch	5	17
WINTON	Mary	3	Forglen	Forglen	4	3
WINTON	William	1	Inverkeithny	Marnoch	5	17
WISELY	Elizabeth	37	Marnoch	Marnoch	5	15
WISEMAN	Charlotte	86	Elgin Mor.	Forglen	2	5
WOOD	Alexander	23	Turriff ABD	Marnoch	3	2
WOOD	Ann	35	Cromdale INV	Marnoch	7	12
WOOD	Ann Moyes?	21	Forglen	Forglen	2	3
WOOD	Catherine	4	Forgue ABD	Inverkeithny	3	2
WOOD	David	2	Marnoch	Marnoch	7	13
WOOD	George	13	Daviot ABD	Marnoch	4	5
WOOD	Isabella	22	Turriff	Forglen	1	7
WOOD	James	55	Forglen	Forglen	2	3
WOOD	Jean	70	Forgue ABD	Marnoch	5	2
WOOD	Margaret	5	Forgue ABD	Marnoch	7	13
WOOD	Mary	65	Alvah	Forglen	2	3
WOOD	Robert	31	Newcastle ENG	Marnoch	7	12
WOOD	Robert	26	Auchterless ABD	Forglen	1	5
WOOD	William	1	Forglen	Forglen	1	7
WOOD	William	27	Auchterless	Forglen	1	7
WRIGHT	Alexandrina	26	Keith	Marnoch	8	8
WRIGHT	Christian	33	Marnoch	Marnoch	8	8
WRIGHT	David	77	Forglen	Forglen	4	4
WRIGHT	James	1	Marnoch	Marnoch	8	8
WRIGHT	Jane	20	Alvah	Marnoch	6	10
WRIGHT	John	46	Deskford	Marnoch	8	8
WRIGHT	John	31	Old Meldrum ABD	Marnoch	8	8
WRIGHT	John	4mths	Marnoch	Marnoch	8	1
WRIGHT	William	3	Marnoch	Marnoch	8	8
WRIGHT	male	1 day	Marnoch	Marnoch	8	9
YEATS	Agnes	50	Fyvie ABD	Inverkeithny	3	5
YEATS	Ann	9	Auchterless ABD	Inverkeithny	3	5
YEATS	James	17	Auchterless ABD	Inverkeithny	3	5
YEATS	James	47	Auchterless ABD	Inverkeithny	3	5
YEATS	Jane	15	Auchterless ABD	Inverkeithny	3	5
YEATS	Peter	4	Inverkeithny	Inverkeithny	3	5
YOUNG	Jane	62	Forglen	Marnoch	5	12
YOUNG	Janet	58	Rothes mOR	Marnoch	1	8
YOUNG	Jean	7	Auchterless ABD	Forglen	2	2
YOUNG	Margaret	25	Monquhitter ABD	Forglen	2	2
YOUNG	Mary	32	Forglen	Marnoch	5	12
YOUNG	Theodore	22	Rothiemay	Forglen	2	2
YOUNG	Thomas	67	Inverurie ABD	Marnoch	1	8

SURNAME	CHR. NAME	AGE	BIRTH PLACE	CENSUS PARISH	BOOK	PG
YOUNG	Walter	31	Rothiemay	Forglen	2	2
YOUNGSON	James	50	King Edward ABD	Marnoch	6	6
YOUNGSON	James	10	Marnoch	Marnoch	6	6
YOUNGSON	Margaret	50	Alvah	Marnoch	6	6
YOUNGSON	William	7	Marnoch	Marnoch	6	6